Guide to Growing Herbs

A comprehensive guide to every aspect of natural herb gardening

Guide to Growing Herbs

A comprehensive guide to every aspect of natural herb gardening

Lori Trojan

Guide to Growing Herbs

A comprehensive guide to every aspect of natural herb gardening including designing a garden, growing, nurturing and harvesting herbs, identifying over 50 herb varieties and using them for decorative, culinary, aromatherapy and medicinal purposes.

Copyright © 2021 by Lori Trojan

All rights reserved. No part of this publication may be reproduced, distributed, or transmitted in any form or by any means, including photocopying, recording, or other electronic or mechanical methods, without the prior written permission of the copyright holder, except in the case of brief quotations embodied in critical reviews and certain other noncommercial uses permitted by copyright law. For permission requests, write to the publisher, addressed "Attention: Permissions Coordinator," at the address below.

ISBN: 978-1-64318-072-4

Published by

Distributed by

703 Eighth Street
Baldwin City, KS, 66006
www.imperiumpublishing.com

Wild Ivy Herb Farm
Lawrence, KS 66046 USA

Please seek the help of a medical professional for medical problems as the information in this guidebook has not been evaluated by the U.S. Food and Drug Administration (FDA) and is not intended to diagnose, treat, cure or prevent any disease.

All rights reserved worldwide www.wildivyherbfarm.com

Wild Ivy Herb Farm

Wild Ivy Herb Farm is a 3 acre labor of love located in Lawrence, KS.

Our mission is to use sustainable permaculture strategies in cultivating non-GMO medicinal, kitchen and native herbs using organic methods. We offer education about growing herbs and how to prepare and utilize them in a multitude of formats. Each year, workshops are conducted on the farm about various topics including organic gardening, making herbal medicines and sustainable lifestyle practices.

Please visit
www.wildivyherbfarm.com to learn more about growing herbs, product offerings and educational opportunities

Table of Contents

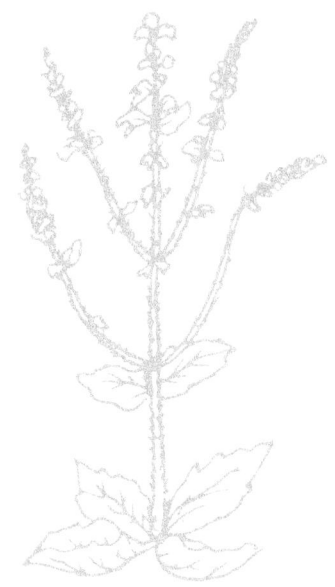

9	Introduction
12	Purpose
14	Identifying and Preparing a Site to Plant Herbs
22	Varieties of Herbs
30	Characteristics of Herbs
76	Designing a Decorative Herb Garden
84	Companion Planting
94	Care and Maintenance of the Herb Garden
102	Perennials, Annuals & Growing from Seed
108	Harvesting, Drying & Freezing Herbs
114	Tinctures, Teas, Infusions, Decoctions, Syrups, Salves, Oils & Vinegars
128	Decorating With Herbs
140	Frequently Asked Questions

Guide to Growing Herbs

Introduction

From the time I was 8, I spent most summers with my Grandparents at their small cottage-like home in western Missouri. I remember it as an enchanting place surrounded by thick fruit brambles and wild gardens brimming with intriguing rare and mysterious herbs. My Grandparents used a variety of natural and organic methods in their gardens. There was no choice to do otherwise as today's chemical pesticides and fertilizers did not exist.

Companion planting, regular weeding and rotating plant varieties were but a few methods used to keep the gardens healthy.

Grandma respected and honored the plants as if they were human. I watched as she communed with them; sometimes humming, sometimes singing as she nurtured and encouraged each one to flourish. She was as unique as the plants themselves. A humble medicine woman whose wisdom had been instilled by generations of natural healers. She had been taught the secrets of preparing herbal salves, liniments, ointments, syrups, lozenges, tonics, tinctures, teas and more.

My Grandma, her Mother before her and hers before her had been the "Doctors" in their village for generations before degreed medical professionals were trusted. Big pharmaceutical companies did not exist then as they do now.

Grandma was one of eight children in a family that arrived in America when she was 16 years old. They had roots deeply embedded in European soil for centuries before they escaped their oppressive life in search of freedom and opportunity.

They brought treasured rare medicinal plant seeds and vast knowledge of their uses along with them on their journey. My ancestors continued to keep their old-world traditions alive which included making natural herbal remedies for family members, friends and neighbors.

Along with medicine-making, Grandma delighted in creating and sharing hand-made herbal body creams, oils and perfumes. She taught me so many things over the years. A herb that could heal a burn by rejuvenating skin cells could also reduce the signs of aging. Yet another could season a chicken for dinner, add shine as a hair rinse or could be pressed into an oil to keep rodents away.

Her vast knowledge of uses and preparations for simple plants seemed magical and endless. Grandma instilled in me a knowledge and love of the herbs that had sustained the health of our family for generations.

Today at Wild Ivy Herb Farm I aspire to honor the memory of my beloved Grandmother by cultivating a vast variety of culinary and medicinal herbs. In addition, we create natural herbal products from family recipes centuries old along with a few new recipes of our own!

I am Lori Trojan, Master Herbalist, Master Gardener, Author, Educator, Farmer, Mother and Grandmother. I have a deep love for the land and all plants native and natural. My greatest passions are supporting sustainable natural farming, Fair Trade practices, the use of non-GMO seeds, seed saving and educating as many people as possible about the growing techniques, properties, uses and preparations of herbs.

Wild Ivy Herb Farm in Lawrence, Kansas also hosts educational workshops and community gatherings. I hope to see you on the farm!

May this Guide to Growing Herbs bring you success in the design, planting and nurturing of your own unique and magical herb garden.

I wish you love, laughter, peace and above all, good health!

Forever Grateful
Lori Trojan
Steward, Wild Ivy Herb Farm

Purpose

The purpose of this guidebook is to partner with you in designing, planting and growing a successful herb garden. It will also assist in identifying those herbs you wish to grow. It is my hope that a herb garden will only be the beginning of your adventure as you discover all the wondrous things you can do with herbs within these pages!

In this Guidebook you will find:
- Latin names, growth habits, flower colors, foliage description, parts to harvest and when to harvest over 50 well-known herbs.
- Culinary, medicinal and aromatherapy properties of these herbs plus preferred preparations and cautions for each, if any.
- Instructions for harvesting, preserving, drying and freezing herbs to use for a multitude of purposes.
- Step-by-step methods to prepare tinctures, teas, infusions, decoctions, syrups, salves, infused oils and vinegars.
- How-to tips for home decorating and crafting.

Whatever your reason for cultivating herbs, whether for kitchen use or health benefits, for color pops and texture in your landscape, for companion planting in a vegetable garden or any number of additional reasons, this guide should help you to better understand the complexity of the humble herb.

Identifying & Preparing a Site to Plant Herbs

No garden is truly complete without an assortment of kitchen and medicinal herbs. Medicinals are of primary importance as they may help to maintain and improve the health of you and your family naturally. Unique herb plants tend to be more difficult to find in your local nursery or garden center which is an excellent reason to grow your own from seed. Cut fresh kitchen herbs are widely available now in most groceries, but to buy them in quantity can become quite expensive.

Whether you have a vast outdoor garden and can dedicate large spaces to herb cultivation or you are growing in pots outside or in, herbs will be the most important plants you will ever grow. For example, Valerian may be an aid for those with sleep disorders. Feverfew can be an important ally in treating tension or migraine headaches. Both these plants may be difficult to find in your local market. So, if you have a limited growing space, grow herbs!

Identifying an Appropriate Planting Site

Begin by looking for a patch of ground that gets full sun at least 4 hours per day. Most herbs thrive in full sunlight, fewer prefer shade. When assessing the viability of an area for planting, keep in mind that during the winter, trees are barren of leaves. In spring and summer those bare branches will have an abundance of leaves, potentially causing your garden area to be shaded. Imagine what the area will look like in the spring before committing that space to growing herbs.

Containers (from pots to raised beds) can be used in the growing area as well as planting directly into the ground and often this dual system can allow for additional growing space. Consider the options as you decide.

As for the size of your garden, it is only limited by the land you have available to use!

If possible, choose an area that is near the house or visible from it. When the garden is within your sight, it is a constant reminder to care for it. Being close to the house also makes it easily accessible for regular harvesting. A window view can contribute to your sense of well-being. It will be a constant source of satisfaction to look out and observe the beauty and success of your efforts.

Growing Conditions

- Good drainage
- Full sun exposure
- Neutral to alkaline soil

Providing these three basic growing conditions is ideal to ensure a healthy and abundant crop. Several popular kitchen herbs (thyme, sage, oregano, rosemary, and more) originate from the Mediterranean and therefore love the natural growing conditions of that region - hot dry summers and cool wet winters. They can also adapt to various climates needing little water in summer with an ability to overwinter if well mulched.

Soil Preparation

If possible, prepare the soil about 1-2 months ahead of planting time or in the fall before spring planting. Spring planting time is usually just after the last frost of the year has passed.

First, remove all grass and weeds from your herb garden site. Try to do this the day after a nice rain when the soil voluntarily releases the roots of the weeds to be removed. It makes the task much simpler when working in rhythm with Mother Nature instead of working against Her. Keeping garden beds weed free is vitally important so herbs are not fighting uninvited plants for root space and water.

Next, gently dig the soil with a hoe or tiller allowing any possible future frosts to help break up and soften the ground.

Soil ph should be neutral, ideally 6-6.5. If you are unsure of the ph balance of your soil, simple test kits are available at most garden centers. Your local County Extension office should also provide soil testing for a minimal fee. Once you have your test results, add any components needed to achieve as close to neutral, bordering on alkaline, as possible before planting. If you have a clay soil, adding lime will help to balance ph. Some woody varieties like lavender, rosemary and bay prefer more gritty soil.

Soil with good drainage is essential as herbs generally don't like "wet feet". They can be prone to root rot from too much water if soil does not drain well. The majority of herbs thrive in typical garden soil with good drainage. If you have areas of standing water, dig about 6-8 inches down and add a layer of small gravel that will sit below the roots to accommodate better drainage. Adding small rocks is more effective than adding sand. If there is a high clay component to your soil, the result of adding sand will cause the soil to be more like concrete than loam.

Herbs survive and thrive with low nutrient needs so feeding with fertilizer is unnecessary. Mulch or compost can be added to soil with a view to better drainage, not for additional nutrients. Late fall or early spring is the time to add well-rotted organic matter like mushroom compost or your own homemade compost. Using manure as a fertilizer for herbs can be too rich and will often produce over-sensitive plants that are not cold-hardy and have little aroma.

Please note that if you don't have the time to test or pre-prep soil, don't let that keep you from planting. Herbs are less fussy than most other plants. In fact, most medicinal herbs are classified as "weeds" and we know how weeds can flourish! Soil can also continue to be improved throughout the season with compost, mulch, etc. if needed.

Containers and Impeding Spread

As "weeds", herbs like mint, lemon balm, catnip, tansy and woodruff tend to spread in an effort to dominate the garden. Bury buckets or large pots with drainage holes in the ground up to the rim and plant these greedy herbs in the pots. This will keep them from a "hostile" take-over, suffocating others. Each spring, consider replacing the soil in these pots to help replenish nutrients. Spring is the ideal time to plant herbs in containers though they can be planted year round. Water the herbs well before planting and leave enough room between plants for each one to spread and develop. It is best to use a potting mix that holds moisture but allows for good drainage. Try combining 1/3 composted soil, 1/3 peat moss or coconut coir and 1/3 perlite. Water again after planting to settle the soil around the roots. Now stand back and let Mother Nature take over.

Lori Trojan

Varieties of Herbs

Following is a reference guide to 50 common varieties of herbs including their Latin names, annual (plant yearly), perennial (comes back yearly), biennial (lasts about 2 years), height & spread width (where applicable), description of flowers and foliage, parts to harvest and when to harvest.

Varieties of Herbs

Herb	Type	Height & Width	Flowers	Foliage	Parts to Harvest	When to Harvest
ANGELICA *Angelica archangelica*	biennial	60-100 x 36 in. 150-250 x 90 cm.	Green/white	2-3 x pinnate, finely toothed	leaves, seeds, stems, rhizomes	summer
ARNICA *Arnica montana*	perennial	12 -24 in. 30 x 60 cm.	yellow	opposite, hair-like	flowers	fully open flowers
BASIL (Sweet) *Ocimum basilicum*	annual	10-24 x 12 in. 25-60 x 30 cm.	white/purple aromatic	oblong	leaves, stems	growing season
BAY (Sweet) *Laurus nobilis*	perennial	26-13 ft. 800-400 cm.	cream/yellow aromatic	thick, leathery	leaves	growing season prune before frost
BERGAMOT *Monarda didyma*	perennial	20-40 x 12 in. 50-100 x 30 cm.	crimson	paired, 4-6", long, aromatic	leaves, stems, roots	growing season roots in fall
BETONY *Stachys officinalis*	perennial	4-24 x 12 in. 10-60 x 30 cm.	purple/red	tooth-edged	flowers, spikes, leaves	growing season
BLACK COHOSH *Cimicifuga racemosa*	perennial	3-6 ft. 1-2 m.	white	tooth-edged	root, rhizome	fall
BLESSED THISTLE *Cnicus benedictus*	annual	27 in. 70 cm.	yellow	downy, prickly	root, seeds, aerial	summer, fall
BORAGE *Borago officinalis*	annual	24-20 in. 60-50 cm.	dk. blue	rough, hairy	flowers, root, leaves	summer
BROOM *Sarothamnus scoparius*	perennial	10 x 7 ft. 300 x 200 cm.	yellow	pointed	flowering tops	growing season
BURDOCK *Arctium lappa*	annual biennial	6 ft.	purple	large, wide	all parts	growing season root in fall

Varieties of Herbs

Herb	Type	Height & Width	Flowers	Foliage	Parts to Harvest	When to Harvest
CARAWAY *Carum carvi*	biennial	32 x 8 in. 80 x 20 cm.	white	feathery	ripe seed	late summer, fall
CELANDINE *Chelidonium majus*	perennial	12-36 x 16 in. 30-90 x 40 cm.	yellow	green/gray	flowering stems	growing season juice is poisonous
(GERMAN) CHAMOMILE *Matricaria chamomilla*	annual	24 x 4 in. 60 x 10 cm.	daisy-like	feathery	flowers	when flowers are fully open
CHERVIL *Anthriscus cerefolium*	annual	28 x 12 in. 70 x 30 cm.	white	delicate, aromatic	young leaves	early summer
CHICKWEED *Stellaria media*	perennial	4-6 in. 10 x 40 cm.	white	lt. green, small	aerial	growing season
CHIVES *Allium schoenoprasum*	perennial	12-20 in. high 30-50 cm. high	purple	thin, grass-like	flowers, leaves	growing season
CLEAVERS *Galium aparine*	annual	4 ft. 120 cm.	white	feathery, thin	aerial	flowers open
COMFREY *Symphytum officinale*	perennial	40 x 32 in. 100 x 80 cm.	cream, pink	lt. green, hairy	leaves, roots	leaves in summer roots in fall
COWSLIP *Primula yeris*	perennial	10 x 8 in. 25 x20 cm.	yellow	wrinkly	flowers, roots, leaves	growing season
DILL *Anethum graveolens*	annual	80 in. high 200 cm. high	yellow	feathery, aromatic	flowers, leaves, seeds	growing season
ELECAMPANE *Inula helenium*	perennial	120 x 40 in. 300 x 100 cm.	yellow	large, lt. green	roots	fall

Varieties of Herbs

Herb	Type	Height & Width	Flowers	Foliage	Parts to Harvest	When to Harvest
EVENING PRIMROSE *Oenothera biennis*	biennial	60 x 24 in. 150 x 60 cm.	yellow	long, pointed, shiny	flowers, roots, seeds	growing season
FENNEL *Foeniculum vulgare*	perennial	80 x 36 in. 200 x 90 cm.	yellow	feathery, aromatic	leaves, stems, seeds	young leaves ripe seed
FENUGREEK *Trigonella foenum-graecum*	annual	20 x 12 in. 50 x 30 cm.	white	trifoliate	leaves, seeds	growing season
FEVERFEW *Tanacetum parthenium*	perennial	12-20 in. high 30-50 cm. high	daisy-like	lt. green, aromatic	leaves, flowers	summer
FOXGLOVE *Digitalis purpurea*	biennial	80 in. high 200 cm. high	white, purple	grey/green, soft, large	leaves	growing season poisonous
GARLIC *Allium sativum*	perennial	12 in. high 30 cm. high	white	pointed, flat	flowers, leaves, roots	fall
GOLDEN SEAL *Hydrastis canadensis*	perennial	12 x 10 in. 30 x 25 cm.	white	fine tooth, 5-7 lobes	rhizome, root	fall
HOREHOUND (WHITE) *Marrubium vulgare*	perennial	24 x 20 in. 60 x 50 cm.	white	grey/green, flowering stem	leaves	when in bud
HORSERADISH *Armoracia rusitcana*	perennial	80 in. high 200 cm. high	insignificant	large, coarse	roots, leaves	leaves in spring roots in fall
HYSSOP *Hyssopus officinalis*	perennial	20 x 16 in. 50 x 40 cm.	blue, pink, white, purple	dk. green, aromatic	leaves	before flowers open
LADY'S MANTLE *Alchemilla vulgaris*	perennial	20 x 16 in. 50 x 40 cm.	greenish yellow	green, round	leaves	summer

Varieties of Herbs

Herb	Type	Height & Width	Flowers	Foliage	Parts to Harvest	When to Harvest
LAVENDER *Lavendula officinalis*	perennial	32 x 24 in. 80 x 60 cm.	mauve, purple	grey/green, narrow	flowers	summer
LEMON BALM *Melissa officinalis*	perennial	32 x 24 in. 80 x 60 cm.	white/pink	aromatic	leaves	growing season
LEMON VERBENA *Lippia citriodora*	perennial	80 x 40 in 200 x 100 cm.	pale lavender	lt. green, aromatic	leaves	growing season
LILY OF THE VALLEY *Convallaria majalis*	perennial	4-8 in. high 10-20 cm.	white	wide, flat, pointed	flowers	when in bloom poisonous to ing
LOVAGE *Levisticum officinale*	perennial	80 x 40 in. 200 x 100 cm.	green/yellow	large, scented	seeds, leaves, roots	fall
LUNGWORT *Pulmonaria officinalis*	perennial	12 x 14 in. 30 x 35 cm.	red, purple	oval, pointed, white spots	whole plant	when flowers op
MARIGOLD *Calendula officinalis*	annual	20 x 10 in. 50 x 25 cm.	orange, yellow, red, single, double	grey/green	flowers	when open and d
MARJORAM *Origanum majorana*	perennial	10-20 x 10 in. 25-50 x 25 cm.	white, pink	greyish, aromatic	leaves, flowering stems	growing season
MARSHMALLOW *Althea officinalis*	perennial	40-80 x 36 in. 100-200 x 90 cm.	large, pink	large, grey/green	flowers, leaves, roots	fall
MEADOWSWEET *Filipendula ulmaria*	perennial	24-36 x 12 in. 60-90 x 30 cm.	cream	dk. green	flower heads, roots	fall
MOTHERWORT *Leonurus cardiaca*	perennial	48 x 24 in. 120 x 60 cm.	pink	whorled on spikes	aerial parts, stems	growing season

Varieties of Herbs

Herb	Type	Height & Width	Flowers	Foliage	Parts to Harvest	When to Harvest
MULLEIN *Verbascum thapsus*	biennial	7 ft. high 200 cm. high	yellow	grey/green, large, soft	flowers, leaves	growing season
NETTLE, STINGING *Urtica dioica*	perennial	3-6 ft. 90-180 cm.	white	tooth-edged, stinging	aerial	growing season
PANSY (WILD) *Viola tricolor*	annual biennial	4-6 x 8 in. 10-15 x 20 cm.	violet, yellow	sparse	flowers	growing season
PARSLEY *Petroselinum crispum*	biennial	24 x 16 in. 60 x 40 cm.	greenish yellow	dk. green, curled	leaves, seed, root	growing season
PEPPERMINT *Mentha piperata*	perennial	12-20 in. high 30-50 cm. high	mauve	shiny, green/purple	leaves, flowers	growing season
PURSLANE *Portulaca oleracea*	perennial	12-16 lin. high 30-40 cm.	yellow	thick, smooth	leaves	growing season
ROSEMARY *Rosmarinus officinalis*	perennial	68 in. high 70 cm. high	blue	thin, grey/green, aromatic	leaves	growing season
RUE *Ruta graveolens*	perennial	24 x 16 in. 60 x 40 cm.	yellow	green/blue, aromatic	leaves	growing season
SAGE *Salvia officinalis*	perennial	12-24 x 20 in. 30-60 x 50 cm.	violet/blue pink/white	grey/green, soft, scented	leaves	growing season
SAW PALMETTO *Serenoa serrulata*	perennial	3-6 ft. 90-180 cm	berries	fan-like	berries	ripened berries
SKULLCAP *Scutellaria lateriflora*	perennial	24 in. high 60 cm. high	blue	yellow/green	whole plant	before flowering

Varieties of Herbs

Herb	Type	Height & Width	Flowers	Foliage	Parts to Harvest	When to Harvest
SHEPHERD'S PURSE *Capsella bursa-pastoris*	annual	1 ft. 30 cm.	insignificant	long, lobed	aerial	growing season
SOAPWORT *Saponaria officinalis*	perennial	16 x 24 in. 40 x 60 cm.	pink single, double	lt. green	leaves, root	leaves in summer roots in fall
TANSY *Tanacetum vulgare*	perennial	48 in. high 120 cm. high	yellow	feathery, aromatic	leaves	before flowers open
TARRAGON (FRENCH) *Artemisia dranunculus*	perennial	36 x 24 in. 90 x 60 cm.	white, insignificant	thin, green, shiny	leaves	spring to summer
VALERIAN *Valeriana officinalis*	perennial	8 in.–5 ft. 20 cm.-1.5 m.	white, aromatic	pinnate	root	fall
VERVAIN *Verbena officinalis*	perennial	1-3 ft. 30-90 cm.	blue spikes	lobed	aerial	growing season
VIOLET, SWEET *Viola adorata*	annual	4-6 x 4 in. 10-15 x 10 cm.	pink, violet, white	dk. green, oval	flowers, leaves, roots	early spring
WOODRUFF *Asperula odorata*	perennial	10 in. high 25 cm. high	white	whorled	flowers, leaves	growing season
WORMWOOD *Artemisia absinthium*	perennial	2-3 ft. high 60-90 cm. high	insignificant	lt. green, fernlike	leaves	growing season poisonous
YELLOW DOCK *Rumex crispus*	perennial	20-40 in. 50-100 cm.	insignificant	long, green	root	fall

Lori Trojan

Characteristics of Herbs

Understanding the many characteristics and uses of each herb you plant is important. Not only will you enjoy the beauty and aroma of your garden, you will be able to utilize your herbs in ways that will astound you! Following is information regarding each one's aromatherapy, culinary uses, medicinal uses, properties, preparations and cautionary guidelines.

ANGELICA

Culinary:	Candied stems, leaves with fish, fruit, in salads.
Medicinal:	Soothes menstrual pain, coughs, poor circulation, anemia, chest colds, gentle laxative
Properties:	Warming, restorative, pectoral, antiseptic, diuretic, diaphoretic, expectorant, anti-spasmodic, strengthens digestion
Preparations:	Raw, tincture, tea, infusion or decoction, infused oil
Cautions:	Avoid during pregnancy, leaves are better suited for children. Overall use in moderation.

ARNICA

Medicinal:	Only use externally. Use for treating bruises, sprains, muscle and rheumatic pain, skin inflammation.
Properties:	Vulnerary, anti-inflammatory
Preparations:	Salve, lotion, gel, compress, infused oil
Cautions:	Do not use internally without the advice of a homeopathic expert as it can be toxic. Do not use on broken skin.

BASIL

Culinary: Use in moderation, pungent scent and flavoring, used in Greek, Italian, Mexican, American dishes.

Aromatherapy: Inhale to help headaches, fight fatigue, anxiety, depression.

Medicinal: Nerve tonic, natural tranquilizer, assists with concentration, helps headaches, head colds. Fights fatigue, depression, anxiety, aids urinary infections, prostatitis, regulates menstrual cycle, compress for engorged breasts, shrinks warts, relieves snake bites, insect repellent, helps heal mouth ulcers, gum infections.

Properties: Anti-infectious, anti-inflammatory, antibacterial, anti-spasmodic, regulator of Nervous System

Preparations: Raw, tincture, infused oil, mouthwash

Cautions: Use in moderation (there is concern about toxicity in large amounts), if overused can cause depression, avoid use during pregnancy. Not recommended for babies, children.

BAY (SWEET)

Culinary:	Add leaves to stews, casseroles or flavoring sachets.
Aromatherapy:	Use in vaporizer for replenishing and uplifting, aids depression. Pleasant incense.
Medicinal:	When inhaled, acts as a pulmonary antiseptic, aids with common cold, pneumonia, sinusitis, bronchitis. Massage oil into hair to assist growth and strength.
Properties:	antiseptic, anti-depressant, aids digestion, regulates Rheumatic System
Preparations:	Raw, infused oil
Cautions:	Avoid during pregnancy. Not recommended for babies, children.

BERGAMOT

Culinary: Use in candy-making or lozenges, flavoring for Earl Grey tea.

Aromatherapy: Refreshing citrus scent reduces depression, gives uplifting feeling, fights fatigue, calming.

Medicinal: Assists to calm Central Nervous System, restores appetite, combats colic and intestinal disorders, lowers fever, aids in digestion and bronchitis, useful for helping skin conditions like psoriasis, acne, ulcers, scars, herpes, seborrhea of the scalp. Also used to treat hemorrhoids.

Properties: Antiseptic, anti-spasmodic, analgesic, anti-depressant, anti-infectious, antibacterial

Preparations: Tincture, infused oil, salve. Also used in perfumes, soaps, etc.

Cautions: Avoid during pregnancy. Not recommended for babies, children. Oil may cause sunburn.

BETONY

Medicinal:	Strengthens and feeds the Central Nervous System, mild sedative, helps to relieve nervous debility associated with tension and anxiety. Eases nervous headache, especially when combined with Skullcap.
Properties:	Sedative, nervine, tonic, bitter, vulnerary
Preparations:	Tincture, tea, infusion

BLACK COHOSH

Medicinal:	Known for its general ability to enhance the many aspects of the female reproductive system. Treats ovarian cramps, cramps in the womb, painful or delayed menstruation, regulates hormonal imbalance, often used during labor to make it more efficient while reducing nervousness and anxiety. Also treats rheumatic, muscular, neurological and arthritic pain. Reduces coughing spasms.
Properties:	Tonic, nervine, anti-spasmodic, sedative, alterative, emmenagogue.
Preparations:	Tincture, decoction
Cautions:	Avoid during pregnancy up until labor and delivery.

BLESSED THISTLE

Medicinal: Stimulates the flow of bile and gastric secretions to aid in dyspepsia, loss of appetite, indigestion. Can help with diarrhea and hemorrhage.

Properties: Tonic, astringent, expectorant, emmenagogue, galactagogue, diaphoretic, bitter tonic, antibacterial

Preparations: Tincture, tea, infusion

BORAGE

Culinary: Use fresh in salads, candy making, iced tea.

Medicinal: Strengthens and tones the heart, provides a sense of well-being, relieves stress, soothes nerves, aids in athlete's foot, ringworm, yeast infection, strengthens kidney function, mild diuretic. Can insure a plentiful and rich supply of breast milk in nursing mothers, nourishes the adrenals.

Properties: Astringent, anti-fungal, mucilaginous, galactagogue

Preparations: Raw, tincture, tea, infusion, infused oil, syrup

Cautions:	Seed oils can become rancid in minutes; use only freshly ground seed. Hairs of plant could be irritating to the skin. Can contain minute amounts of poisonous alkaloids, therefore use sparingly and do not use for a prolonged period of time.

BROOM

Medicinal:	Associated with the heart and the blood. Increases the efficiency of each beat of the heart while producing peripheral constriction of the blood vessels. Can be used when water retention occurs due to weakness of the heart. Use to reduce heavy blood flow during menses.
Properties:	Cardioactive, diuretic, hypertensive, peripheral vasoconstrictor, astringent
Preparations:	Tincture, tea, infusion
Cautions:	Avoid during pregnancy or hypertension.

BURDOCK

Culinary: The root often called "Gobo" is popular in Asian dishes. Eaten raw, stir-fried and in soups.

Medicinal: Effective long-term treatment of skin conditions which result in dry or scaly skin. Helps restore balance in overall general health when there are outside indicators of imbalance such as dry skin, dry scalp. Has been used to treat anorexia nervosa to aid kidney function. Stimulates bile production, heals cystitis, wounds, ulcers

Properties: Tonic, laxative, digestive bitter, diuretic, vulnerary

Preparations: Tincture, decoction

CARAWAY

Culinary: Seeds often used in bread-making or as a flavoring in any dish.

Medicinal: An aid for children suffering from intestinal colic, calming, eases flatulence and dyspepsia, treats diarrhea and can also be used as a gargle for sore throat and laryngitis, treats bronchitis and bronchial asthma, relieves cramping from menses, increases milk flow in nursing mothers.

Properties:	Carminative, anti-spasmodic, emmenagogue, expectorant, galactagogue, astringent, anti-microbial, aromatic, stimulant
Preparations:	Tincture, tea, infusion

GREATER CELANDINE

Medicinal:	Best known for its use in the treatment of gallbladder and gallstones, stomach pain. Also used for skin tumors, skin infections and treatment of verrucae.
Properties:	Anti-spasmodic, anodyne, cholagogue, purgative, diuretic
Preparations:	Tincture, decoction
Cautions:	At higher doses, this herb is poisonous and can cause strong purging of the digestive tract. Do not use more than 1-2ml. of tincture per day or 1 cup twice per day using only 2 teaspoons of herb or 1 teaspoon of root material in decoction form. It is dangerous to exceed this dose.

CHAMOMILE

Culinary: Drink as a tea for a calming, relaxing, soothing effect.

Medicinal: German or common garden Chamomile can be used interchangeably for virtually the same effect. Safe for use with children as a calming gentle sedative. Used for anxiety or insomnia. Aids with indigestion and gastritis, reduces nasal catarrh, eases flatulence and dyspepsia. Use as a gargle for sore throat or mouth inflammation and as a rinse for sore eyes. Use topically for reducing swelling and healing wounds.

Properties: Sedative, tonic, carminative, anti-spasmodic, anti-inflammatory, antiseptic, vulnerary, diaphoretic, bitter, emmenagogue, nervine

Preparations: Tincture, infusion, salve, steam for inhalation

CHERVIL

Culinary: One of the ingredients in french fines herbes and has a delicate flavor similar to a cross between parsley and anise. Chervil works most effectively when used in food. Always add at the end of cooking for ultimate flavor. Add to soups, stews, sautés. Compliments carrots, corn, peas, spinach, eggs, sorrel, fish, oysters, shallots, béarnaise sauce and as a garnish.
Medicinal: Treats eczema, high blood pressure, gout, kidney stones, dropsy, pleurisy and menstrual problems.
Properties: Diuretic, stimulant, expectorant
Preparations: Raw, tincture

CHICKWEED

Culinary: Can be eaten raw in salad or just by the handful!
Medicinal: Flushes fat and can be a relief for rheumatism. Use externally for cuts, abrasions, itching and mild skin irritations.
Properties: Emollient, vulnerary, anti-rheumatic
Preparations: Raw, tea, infusion, salve, poultice, compress

CHIVES

Culinary: Best known for use in cooking, raw or steamed. The taste is of mild onion. Use raw in salads (stems, tops and flowers) or as a garnish. Add to soups, stews, sauces, vegetable dishes, cheese or meat dishes. Add at last moments of cooking. Green stems can be used to tie bundles of carrots, asparagus, etc. for a decorative flair.

Medicinal: Chives are rich in sulfur oil which helps lower blood pressure (in large quantities).

Properties: Antiseptic

Preparations: Raw, infused oil

CLEAVERS

Medicinal: Also known as "goosegrass." Helps to move lymph when lymphatic system is congested and acts as a diuretic. Used for swollen glands, tonsillitis, adenoid troubles, cystitis, urinary conditions, ulcers, tumors.

Properties: Diuretic, astringent, hepatic, vulnerary, laxative, alterative, tonic, anti-inflammatory, anti-neoplastic, anti-cancer

Preparations: Tincture, tea, infusion

COMFREY

Medicinal: Primarily known for its properties of fast healing of wounds, bruises, broken bones, sprains. Efficient for cracked, dry skin, gastritis, stomach ulcers, arthritis, bunions, bed sores, muscle aches (especially old nagging injuries), dry coughs.

Properties: Mucilaginous, demulcent, emollient, pectoral, vulnerary

Preparations: Best used topically as a cream, salve, liniment, infused oil, compress, tea, infusion

Cautions: Has been shown to cause liver disease in lab rats but no proven link to humans. Use leaves for tea, use roots sparingly or with advice from a homeopathic expert. Be sure wounds are clean before using topically. Comfrey heals quickly and may seal in infection by promoting tissue formation over an unhealed wound.

COWSLIP

Medicinal: Flowers used to treat insomnia, nervous tension and as a tea made for headache.
Properties: Sedative, antispasmodic
Preparations: Tincture, tea, infusion, wine-making, essential and volatile oil.

DILL

Culinary: Mild flavor. Seeds, leaves, stems used raw in salads, fish dishes, sauces, soups, stews, vegetable dishes. Used for making pickles.
Medicinal: Eases flatulence and colic, especially in children. Stimulates the flow of milk in nursing mothers. Chewing the seeds can eliminate bad breath.
Properties: Galactagogue, carminative, antispasmodic, anti-emetic
Preparations: Raw, tincture, tea, infusion

ELECAMPANE

Medicinal: Stimulates digestion and appetite, aids in soothing bronchial coughs especially in children. Helps eliminate catarrh, soothes bronchitis, emphysema, bronchial asthma, tuberculosis.

Properties:	Antitussive, expectorant, anti-microbial, astringent, diaphoretic, anti-catarrhal, emollient, hepatic, tonic, vulnerary, mucilaginous, antibacterial, pectoral
Preparations:	Tincture, tea, infusion

EVENING PRIMROSE

Medicinal:	Soothes skin conditions such as eczema, moderates mood swings, relieves premenstrual and menopausal symptoms, treats Multiple Sclerosis, relieves hemorrhoids, bruises, Rheumatoid Arthritis. High in Essential Fatty Acids (EFAs), especially gammalinoleic acid which is also found in black currant seeds and borage seeds.
Properties:	Anti-inflammatory, cardioactive, anti-depressant
Preparations:	Extracted oil, tea, infusion
Cautions:	Side effects may be headache, skin rash, nausea. Not recommended for epileptics.

FENNEL

Culinary: Seeds and leaves used in baking, soups, stews, fish dishes, pizza, flavoring for Italian sausage, vegetable dishes. Mild licorice flavor.

Medicinal: Best known for the relief of stomach upset as in dyspepsia, flatulence, colic, intestinal problems. Similar to properties of aniseed in calming coughs and bronchitis, increases flow of milk in nursing mothers, eases rheumatic and muscular pain. Treats eye inflammation, conjunctivitis.

Properties: Carminative, anti-spasmodic, galactagogue, stimulant, rubefacient, anti-emetic, expectorant, diaphoretic, hepatic

Preparations: Tincture, tea, infusion

FENUGREEK

Medicinal:	Reduces inflammation in wounds, sores, tumors, fistulas and boils. Aids in healing bronchitis, eases sore throats, soothes digestion, stimulates milk production in nursing mothers, stimulates development of the breasts.
Properties:	Tonic, demulcent, expectorant, galactagogue, emmenagogue, vulnerary, emollient
Preparations:	Tincture, poultice, decoction

FEVERFEW

Medicinal:	Primary aid with migraine headaches, inflammatory arthritis. Helps with painful menses.
Properties:	Anti-inflammatory, uterine stimulant, vaso-dilatory, relaxant, digestive bitter
Preparations:	Use sparingly-very bitter. Use the equivalent of one leaf 1-3 times daily. Tincture, tea, infusion
Cautions:	Avoid during pregnancy-may cause early labor by contracting the womb, may cause mouth ulcers for those with sensitivity.

FOXGLOVE

Medicinal:	This herb is the primary source for Digitalis, the medicinal treatment for the heart. Also treats epilepsy, swollen glands, coughs, increases force of heart contractions, helps reduce blood pressure, improves circulation, reduces edema.
Properties:	cardioactive, diuretic, anti-inflammatory, toxic
Preparations:	I do not recommend using without consulting a physician or homeopathic expert.
Cautions:	Highly toxic. Signs of poisoning may be a strong, slow pulse, blurry vision, dizziness, vomiting, tremors, convulsions, diarrhea. Do not use without medical supervision.

GARLIC

Culinary: Can be used in any type of cooking for robust flavor. Use cloves whole, chopped, crushed or as a paste.

Medicinal: Acts on bacteria, alimentary parasites, and viruses. Used for respiratory infections, bronchitis, catarrh, flu, colds, coughs, asthma, infections, aids digestive tract by supporting growth of natural bacteria and killing pathogenic organisms. Reduces cholesterol and high blood pressure. Treats ringworm and threadworm.

Properties: Vulnerary, antibacterial, antiseptic, anti-microbial, alterative, anti-catarrhal, expectorant, stimulant, hypotensive, diaphoretic, cholagogue, anti-spasmodic, pectoral, anthelmintic, carminative, rubefacient, tonic

Preparations: Raw or capsule form to avoid strong smell or taste

GOLDEN SEAL

Medicinal:	Restores and cleanses mucous membranes in the body, therefore aids the entire digestive system. Particularly useful in breaking up upper respiratory catarrh and is also a tonic for use in uterine conditions. Known to be used in healing earache, conjunctivitis, eczema and ridding the body of ringworm.
Properties:	Astringent, tonic, vulnerary, pectoral, expectorant, hepatic, anti-catarrhal, laxative, bitter, alterative, oxytocic, cholagogue, emmenagogue, laxative
Preparations:	Tincture, tea, infusion
Cautions:	Avoid during pregnancy.

WHITE HOREHOUND

Medicinal:	Treats whooping cough or any cough that is non-productive. Aids bronchitis and digestion. Promotes wound healing.
Properties:	Anti-spasmodic, expectorant, vulnerary, pectoral, stimulant, diaphoretic, bitter digestive
Preparations:	Tincture, tea, infusion

HORSERADISH

Culinary: Use grated or shredded to make sauce or condiment. Can be eaten as a vegetable.
Medicinal: Treats flu, colds, fevers, urinary infections, flatulence, rheumatism, bronchitis. Stimulates digestion.
Properties: Carminative, stimulant, rubefacient, diuretic, mild laxative, hepatic
Preparations: Raw, tea, infusion, poultice

HYSSOP

Medicinal: Treats coughs, catarrh, bronchitis, colds, anxiety, hysteria and petit mal seizures.
Properties: Expectorant, anti-spasmodic, sedative, carminative, diaphoretic, anti-catarrhal, hepatic, vulnerary, tonic, pectoral
Preparations: Tincture, tea, infusion

LADY'S MANTLE

Medicinal: Eases menstrual pain and excessive bleeding, aids with menopausal changes, treats diarrhea and can be used as a gargle for mouth sores, ulcers and laryngitis.
Properties: Diuretic, astringent, anti-inflammatory, emmenagogue, vulnerary
Preparations: Tincture, tea, infusion

LAVENDER

Aromatherapy: Essential oil, volatile oil elicits feelings of relaxation, soothes nerves, anti-depressant.
Medicinal: Eases stress headaches, anti-depressant, gentle strengthening tonic for cases of exhaustion, promotes natural sleep, eases aches/pains of rheumatism, treats burns
Properties: Anti-spasmodic, carminative, anti-depressant, rubefacient, anti-emetic, nervine
Preparations: Infused oil, tea, infusion, salve, liniment

LEMON BALM

Culinary: Flavors soups, salads, drinks including wine-based and iced teas.

Aromatherapy: Essential oil extracted by steam distillation has lemony scent. Eases nervousness, depression, calming and uplifting effect, reduces palpitations.

Medicinal: Aids children who suffer with nightmares and restlessness. Helps with sleeplessness, digestion, nervous palpitations, heart disorders, migraine headaches, neuralgia, tension due to stress, eczema, shingles and other stress-related skin maladies. Regulates the menstrual cycle and therefore, assists in natural birth control. Use in conjunction with Dr. Bach's Rescue Remedy to ease shock or intense sadness due to bereavement.

Properties: Tonic, anti-spasmodic, cardioactive, emmenagogue, pectoral, carminative

Preparations: Raw, tincture, tea, infusion, infused oil, salve, liniment, compress, inhalant

Cautions: Use half the measured amount during pregnancy and for babies and children.

LEMON VERBENA

Culinary:	Strong lemon scent used in refreshing teas, wines, stuffing, preserves and desserts.
Medicinal:	Eases nausea, flatulence and dyspepsia.
Properties:	Anti-emetic, carminative
Preparations:	Raw, tincture, tea, infusion

LILY OF THE VALLEY

Medicinal:	Similar action to Foxglove with similar properties without its potentially devastating toxic effects. Treats heart failure, water retention (dropsy) when associated with the heart, congestive conditions related to the heart.
Properties:	Cardioactive, diuretic
Preparations:	I do not recommend using without consulting a physician or homeopathic expert.
Cautions:	Do not use without medical supervision due to varying toxicity levels.

LOVAGE

Culinary:	Mild celery flavor. Use leaves in soups, stews, fish and vegetable dishes. Use seeds in bread making and baking.
Medicinal:	Digestive tonic, induces sweat, diuretic properties, promotes the onset of menses.
Properties:	Emmenagogue, diuretic, diaphoretic
Preparations:	Raw, tincture, tea, infusion
Cautions:	Avoid during pregnancy, do not use if kidney disease is present.

LUNGWORT

Medicinal:	Treats coughs, bronchitis, upper respiratory infection, catarrh, diarrhea (especially in children), hemorrhoids. Heals cuts, wounds.
Properties:	Expectorant, demulcent, astringent, pectoral, vulnerary
Preparations:	Tincture, tea, infusion, salve

MARIGOLD

Culinary: Beautify a salad by tossing in petals!
Medicinal: Reduces inflammation of the skin, aids in healing wounds, rashes, bruises, strains, burns, scalds. Treats stomach ulcers and gastric upset, indigestion and gall bladder problems. May help with menstrual pain.
Properties: Astringent, emmenagogue, anti-inflammatory, vulnerary, anti-microbial, tonic, cholagogue
Preparations: Tincture, tea, infusion, salve, infused oil, liniment, compress, poultice

MARJORAM

Culinary: Use to flavor any dish, often associated with Italian foods. Pungent aroma and flavor.
Medicinal: Treats colds and flu, with similar medicinal characteristics of Hyssop. Also used as a gargle to heal mouth sores, ulcers and sore throat. Helps with coughs, whooping cough, infections from wounds, tension headaches, muscular and rheumatic pain. Soothes bee stings and bug bites.

Properties:	Diaphoretic, stimulant, expectorant, antimicrobial, emmenagogue, rubefacient
Preparations:	Tincture, tea, infusion, mouthwash, salve, infused oil

MARSHMALLOW

Medicinal:	The root is primarily used for digestive problems and skin conditions as well as varicose veins, boils and abscesses. The leaves are used mainly for the lungs, urinary system, respiratory distress, bronchitis, catarrh and annoying coughs.
Properties:	Root: demulcent, diuretic, emollient, vulnerary. Leaves: expectorant, demulcent, diuretic, emollient, pectoral, anti-catarrhal
Preparations:	Tincture, tea, infusion, decoction, compress, poultice

MEADOWSWEET

Medicinal:	Highly recommended as a digestive remedy. Soothes mucous membranes of the digestive tract, reduces nausea and stomach acid, aids in healing gastric and peptic ulcers including heartburn. Can reduce fever and relieve muscle and joint pain.
Properties:	Anti-inflammatory, anti-emetic, astringent, stomachic, anti-rheumatic
Preparations:	Tincture, tea, infusion

MOTHERWORT

Medicinal:	Useful in the treatment of mood swings from PMS or Menopause and is a woman's support. Eases anxiety and tension, heart strengthener. May be used in heart conditions which stem from anxiety.
Properties:	Emmenagogue, anti-spasmodic, sedative, tonic, nervine, hepatic
Preparations:	Tincture, tea, infusion

MULLEIN

Medicinal: Aids healing and toning of the Respiratory System while reducing inflammation and stimulating fluid production. Helps to clear chesty coughs. Eases bronchitis, sore throat, and any inflammation internally or externally.

Properties: Demulcent, diuretic, expectorant, anti-catarrhal, sedative, vulnerary, pectoral, emollient

Preparations: Tincture, tea, infusion

NETTLE

Culinary: Steamed or boiled, nettles taste similar to spinach when cooked and are quite tasty. High in calcium, minerals and vitamins.

Medicinal: One of the most dependable treatments for overall well-being as well as support for menopausal symptoms and nervousness. Has a calming effect. Useful for hemorrhaging in the body including nose bleeds.

Properties: Rubefacient, alterative, diuretic, tonic, astringent

Preparations: Tincture, tea, infusion

PANSY

Culinary:	Toss flower petals into a salad or as a garnish. Beautiful and delicious!
Medicinal:	Also known as "heartease", treats weeping eczema, coughs, bronchitis, urinary problems, cystitis.
Properties:	Anti-inflammatory, diuretic, expectorant, laxative, anti-rheumatic
Preparations:	Tincture, tea, infusion, infused oil, salve

PARSLEY

Culinary:	Used to add color and flavor as a garnish or ingredient. Reduces bad breath when chewed raw. Notable source of Vitamin C.
Medicinal:	Reduces water retention as a diuretic, stimulates menstruation, eases flatulence and colic pain.
Properties:	Expectorant, carminative, emmenagogue, tonic, diuretic
Preparations:	Raw, tincture, tea, infusion
Cautions:	Avoid during pregnancy.

PEPPERMINT

Culinary: Used to flavor teas, baked goods, candies and chewing gum.

Medicinal: Excellent carminative; stimulates bile production and digestive juice secretion to relieve intestinal problems such as colic and flatulent dyspepsia. Helps relieve travel sickness, vomiting during pregnancy, Crohn's disease, colitis, fevers, colds and flu. Eases tension, stress and anxiety. Helps relieve menstrual pain, itching and inflammation.

Properties: Anti-inflammatory, anti-spasmodic, carminative, nervine, anti-emetic, analgesic, anti-microbial, anti-catarrhal, rubefacient, emmenagogue, stimulant

Preparations: Raw, tincture, tea, infusion, infused oil, essential oil

ROSEMARY

Culinary: Strong flavored and scented, goes well with fish, poultry and vegetable dishes.

Medicinal: Aids digestion, has a stimulating effect on the Circulatory and Nervous System. Used to reduce psychological tension and/or depression, dyspepsia, flatulence, debilitating headache, muscular pain, sciatica and neuralgia. The oil stimulates hair growth.

Properties: Carminative, anti-depressant, anti-spasmodic, anti-microbial, rubefacient, astringent, parasiticide, stimulant, emmenagogue, nervine

Preparations: Raw, tincture, tea, infusion, infused oil, salve, essential oil

PURSLANE

Culinary: Used similarly to spinach and watercress. Lemony flavor, crunchy. High in Vitamin E, fatty acids, beta carotene, Vitamin C, magnesium, riboflavin, potassium and phosphorous.

Medicinal:	Relieves dry cough, shortness of breath, mouth sores, sore gums, inflammation, intestinal worms.
Properties:	Calmative, diuretic, anti-cancer
Preparations:	Raw
Cautions:	Contains oxalates which may inhibit uptake of nutrients, may cause gall or kidney stones.

RUE

Medicinal:	Regulates and brings on menses, powerful abortifacient-do not use during pregnancy. Eases constipation and bowel irritation, increases circulation and lowers blood pressure, relieves headaches, anxiety and palpitations.
Properties:	Emmenagogue, anti-spasmodic, antitussive, abortifacient, anti-microbial, stimulant, anthelmintic, rubefacient, bitter
Preparations:	Raw, tincture, tea, infusion, infused oil
Cautions:	Avoid during pregnancy.

SAGE

Culinary: Used to flavor stuffing, fish and poultry dishes, vegetable and meat dishes, baked goods

Aromatherapy: Often used as an inhalant to soothe mucus membranes. Used in incense and smudge sticks.

Medicinal: Most often used in the treatment of sore gums, mouth, tongue, throat and tonsils. Aids in healing laryngitis, tonsillitis and pharyngitis. Reduces sweating and reduces milk production in nursing mothers. Promotes healing of wounds. Stimulates uterine muscles-do not use if pregnant.

Properties: Carminative, astringent, anti-catarrhal, emmenagogue, anti-microbial, stimulant, febrifuge

Preparations: Raw, tincture, mouthwash, tea, infusion, infused oil, steam for inhalation

Cautions: Avoid during pregnancy.

SAW PALMETTO

Medicinal: Best known for its ability to strengthen and tone the male reproductive system. Used as a treatment for prostate problems, regulates male hormones, may be of value in treating disorders of the gastro-urinary tract.
Properties: Urinary, diuretic, antiseptic, endocrine agent
Preparations: Tincture, decoction

SHEPHERD'S PURSE

Medicinal: A gentle diuretic and astringent for treatment of diarrhea, wounds, nose bleeds, and excessive menstrual bleeding.
Properties: Diuretic, uterine stimulant, vulnerary, astringent
Preparations: Tincture, tea, infusion

SKULLCAP

Medicinal:	Best known for its powerful nervine properties. Relaxes nervous tension, revives the Central Nervous System, treats seizures, hysteria and Epilepsy. Anti-depressant that doubles as anti-fatigue. Can ease pre-menstrual syndrome.
Properties:	Anti-spasmodic, analgesic, nervine, tonic, hypnotic, sedative
Preparations:	Tincture, tea, infusion

SOAPWORT

Medicinal:	In large doses, works as a laxative and can cause upset stomach. Relieves eczema and similar skin conditions. Effective expectorant for coughs and Bronchitis. May also have an effect in aiding gallstones.
Properties:	Laxative, expectorant, diuretic
Preparations:	Tincture, decoction

TANSY

Medicinal:	Best known for its ability to rid the digestive system of roundworms or threadworms. Eases dyspepsia and also stimulates menstruation.
Properties:	Vermifuge, carminative, emmenagogue, anthelmintic, stimulant, digestive bitter
Preparations:	Tincture, tea, infusion
Cautions:	Avoid during pregnancy.

TARRAGON

Culinary:	A mildly sweet flavor reminiscent of licorice used in french fines herbes, dressings, salads, vinegars, poultry, fish and vegetable dishes where a mild flavor is desired.
Medicinal:	Very rarely used medicinally at this time in history though it was once known for its ability to treat toothache.
Preparations:	Raw

SWEET VIOLET

Aromatherapy: A lovely light sweet scent to give an overall feeling of well-being.
Culinary: Toss petals raw in salads or as a garnish, use to flavor honey, candies or sweets
Medicinal: Best known for its use in aiding coughs and bronchial congestion with upper respiratory catarrh. Treats skin conditions and rheumatism as well as urinary infections and is known by many as an anti-cancer treatment
Properties: Anti-inflammatory, diuretic, alterative, expectorant, anti-neoplastic
Preparations: Raw, tincture, tea, infusion

VALERIAN

Medicinal:	The strongest sedative known to the herbal world. Reduces stress, anxiety, hysteria. Treats insomnia. Aids in the relief of cramping; menstrual, intestinal or otherwise. Can also help with rheumatic pain and migraine pain.
Properties:	Sedative, hypnotic, hypotensive, anti-spasmodic, nervine, carminative
Preparations:	Tincture, tea, infusion

VERVAIN

Medicinal:	Nervous System tonic and strengthener. Eases depression, melancholy, listlessness, seizure and mild hysteria. Also effective in treatment of gall bladder, jaundice and gum disease. Fever reducer.
Properties:	Sedative, diaphoretic, nervine tonic, anti-spasmodic, analgesic, hepatic, anti-bilious, emmenagogue, pectoral, expectorant, galactagogue
Preparations:	Tincture, tea, infusion

WOODRUFF

Aromatherapy: Used as a main ingredient in some potpourris and sachets. Recognized for its sweet scent which is similar to newly mowed hay and vanilla. Often used as an ingredient in room fresheners and perfumes.

Culinary: Most often used in beverages. Makes a delicious tea and is often used in wine making.

Medicinal: Once considered to be a wound healer, heart regulator, relaxant and soother of upset stomach. Now mostly used for its scent.

Properties: Calmative, diuretic, diaphoretic, antispasmodic

Preparations: Tea, infusion

Cautions: The U.S. Food and Drug Administration has deemed Woodruff safe only for use in alcoholic beverages as large quantities have been reported to cause dizziness and vomiting.

WORMWOOD

Medicinal: Stimulates and aids the digestive system and like Tansy, rids the body of worms. In this case, roundworms and pinworms. May also reduce fevers and infections. Known as a general body tonic.

Properties: Anti-microbial, carminative, anti-inflammatory, anti-bilious, anthelmintic, bitter tonic, hepatic, emmenagogue, stimulant

Preparations: Tincture, as a powder in capsule form (avoids bitter taste), tea, infusion

YELLOW DOCK

Medicinal: Best known for its use as a skin treatment for eczema, psoriasis and the like. Also aids with constipation, stimulates the flow of bile and is often referred to as a "blood cleanser". Treats jaundice when due to congestion.

Properties: Tonic, laxative, alterative, hepatic, cholagogue

Preparations: Tincture, decoction

Definitions of Properties

ALTERATIVE: Once known as "blood cleaners", these herbs restore balance, function and overall well-being

ANALGESIC/ANODYNE: Herbs that reduce pain

ANTHELMINTIC: Herbs that can expel worms

ANTI-BILIOUS: Can remove excess bile, and help with jaundice conditions

ANTI-CATARRHAL: Help the body eliminate excess catarrh or phlegm

ANTI-EMETIC: Reduce or prevent vomiting

ANTI-INFLAMMATORY: Reduce inflammation, swelling

ANTI-LITHIC: Prevents formation and build-up of stones, gravel in Urinary System

ANTI-MICROBIAL: Assists in destroying and preventing pathogenic micro organisms

ANTI-SPASMODIC: Prevents or eases cramping or spasms

ASTRINGENT: Herbs that help contract tissue, reduce secretions and discharges

BITTER: Due to bitter taste, these herbs stimulate the Digestive System through a reflex via the taste buds

Definitions of Properties

CARDIAC TONIC/ CARDIOACTIVE: Affecting the Heart

CARMINITIVE: Stimulate peristalsis of the Digestive System, relaxing the stomach, aiding digestion. High in volatile oils

CHOLAGOGUE: Stimulate secretion of bile, aiding the gallbladder, laxative effect on the Digestive System

DEMULCENT: Mucilaginous herbs that soothe inflamed internal tissues

DIAPHORETIC: Eliminate toxins and stimulate sweating through perspiration

DIURETIC: Increase elimination of urine

EMETIC: Causes vomiting

EMMENAGOGUE: Normalize and/or stimulate menstrual blood flow

EMOLLIENT: Soften, soothe and protect skin

EXPECTORANT: Remove excess mucous from the Respiratory System

FEBRIFUGE: Reduce fever

GALACTAGOGUE: Increase the flow of milk in nursing mothers

Definitions of Properties

HEPATIC: Strengthen, tone and affect the liver and increase flow of bile

HYPNOTIC: Induce sleep (does not cause a trance state)

LAXATIVE: Promote bowel movement

NERVINE: Tone, strengthen and affect the Nervous System. Can be either a relaxant or stimulant

OXYTOCIC: Stimulate uterine contractions

PECTORAL: Tone, strengthen, affect the Respiratory System

RUBEFACIENT: Stimulate dilation of capillaries thereby increasing circulation by applying externally, aids internal function

SEDATIVE: Calms the Nervous System, reduces tension and stress, induces sleep

STIMULANT: Quicken the physiological functions of the body

TONIC: Strengthens, tones and supports overall systems and organs

VULNERARY: Herbs applied externally to promote healing of wounds

HERBAL REMEDIES DISCLAIMER

The information contained herein is only advisory. While every endeavor has been made to ensure the information contained herein is accurate and correct, no warranties of any kind are made with regard to the completeness and accuracy of the content. No liability whatsoever can be accepted for any condition or adverse reaction which may result from using herbal preparations. The content herein is not meant to be a substitute for authoritative medical supervision or advice. Nor is it intended to be a substitute for consultation with a physician, in relation to any symptoms that may require diagnosis and medical attention. Some herbs interact with prescription drugs and anyone using prescribed or over-the-counter medications should always consult with a doctor or pharmacist before taking herbal preparations.

Designing a Decorative Herb Garden

Whether beginning a floral, vegetable or herb garden, you should always draw your plan on paper before planting in real-time. Consider how much space you have to work with, which plants you wish to incorporate, and what their growing habits are (spreading, climbing, bushy, short, tall, etc.).

When you plant, use your plan as a guide and reminder so all herbs are integrated accordingly. Herb gardens range from free-flow and wild to symmetrical and formal. Design an herb garden that will delight YOU! Once you have created your design and planting plan on paper (see some ideas for plans below), it is time to transfer your design to the planting site. You might use stakes and string or sand to mark the areas of planting. These are all easily removed after planting.

Walking and Decorative Pathways

If you wish to incorporate paths, decorative stones or ornaments, these should usually be placed before planting. Walking paths tend to require heavier materials such as bricks, paving stones or gravel and these could damage the delicate newly-planted root systems of your herbs if not laid first. If using walking pathways, be sure these effectively allow you easy access to maintain and harvest your herbs.

Walking paths, if you have the space for them, are wonderful as they keep you from compacting the soil around your plants by walking on it. However, if your design incorporates decorative paths for visual effect only, they may be placed after planting as lightweight materials such as shredded bark or colored stones won't damage tender new roots. Also, when laying decorative paths through the herb garden, utilize retaining boards or similar to keep path material from falling onto your plants.

Evaluate Before Planting

After your design is marked out on the site, place the herbs (while still in their pots) on the location where they will be permanently planted. This is a good time to re-evaluate and make any changes before digging. This is also the time to place ornamental stones or objects.

Water the herbs well before planting and water again after they go into the soil. Herbs can grow very quickly, so if you only plant one of each variety or if you are starting from seed, it won't be long before they spread and your garden looks lush. If you place more than one plant of each variety together in a small area, your garden will look full but you may limit the space in which your herbs can spread.

Designs and Placement Planning

Following are some suggestions of herb garden designs and placement plans. These may provide some inspiration if you choose to create a more symmetrical, semi-formal or formal garden. If you opt for the "wild" garden, just plant in your designated site area and let Mother Nature do the rest. Herbs can always be separated and replanted after they have had a few seasons to settle in and spread, so you can always (somewhat) control even the wildest garden!

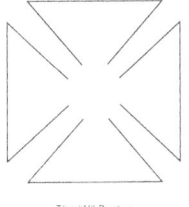
The "X" Design

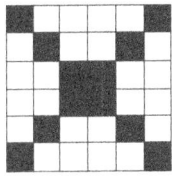
The "Checkerboard" Design

The "X" and the "Checkerboard") are typical examples of symmetrical patterns with unlimited choices of how to plant.

The "X" design demonstrates how walking paths can be used to easily access the plants for maintenance and harvesting. It also allows plenty of room to plant many different varieties by categories. The "Checkerboard" allows for paths, decorative or walking, and plants can be placed in every other square or in any number of patterns.

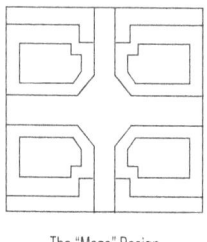 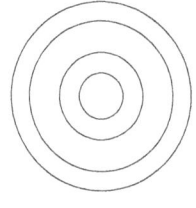

The "Maze" Design   The "Circular" or "Spiral" Design

The "Maze" design allows for a more formal English type of herb garden where hedges might be grown as borders. One large or four small centerpieces can be used. This design also allows for a maze effect which can for example, lead the visitor past a hedge into the center where a bench waits to give rest. Each of the four quadrants could be a different color variety, or categorize by usage (kitchen, medicinal, aromatherapy, etc.). This design allows for great creativity.

The final design example, the "Circular" or "Spiral" also gives the option to plant by category and tends toward a softer, more magical feel. This design lends itself well to planting by height (taller to the outside, moving towards the center where there might be a bench or sculpture surrounded by ground cover herbs). Better still, get creative and design your own plan that has particular significance and meaning to you.

Choosing Herbs

Choosing which varieties of herbs to plant in your garden should be a fun and educational process. Get to know each one and understand why each would be useful to you specifically. Choose for color, kitchen use, medicinal purpose, fragrance, etc. The more you familiarize yourself with each one by observing its growing needs, habits, scent, taste, feel and medicinal power, the more you will feel the connection between yourself and all living things. Gardening connects us to the Earth. Mother Nature empowers us with a sense of satisfaction, purpose, self-sufficiency and self-reliance.

Following are ideas for grouping herb plantings by commonalities:

Kitchen Herbs
Basil
Sage
Parsley
Chives
Thyme
Rosemary
Mint
Lemon Balm
Borage
Oregano
Dill
Bay
Marjoram
Cilantro
Tarragon
Summer Savory

Medicinal Herbs
Valerian
Comfrey
Yarrow
Nettle
Feverfew
Burdock
Mullein
Elecampane
Purple Coneflower
Chamomile
Wood Betony
St. John's Wort
Motherwort
Mugwort
Marigold
Cleavers

Fragrance
Lavender
Sweet Violet
Lemon Thyme
Beebalm
Rosemary
Scented Geranium
Bergamot
Garlic Chives
Catnip (Catmint)
Chocolate Mint
Rose
Tansy
Wormwood
Chervil
Pineapple Sage
Fennel

White
Anise
Blood Root
Caraway
Lily of the Valley
Queen Anne's Lace
Solomon's Seal

Red
Crimson Clover
Poppy
Red Valerian
Red Bergamot
Pleurisy Root
Red Sage

Blue/Purple
Borage
Hyssop
Larkspur
Chicory
Columbine
Flax
Comfrey

Yellow
Agrimony
Broom
Blessed Thistle
Dandelion
Primrose
Sunflower

Grey
Clary Sage
Horehound
Marshmallow
Eucalyptus
Rue (blue/grey)
Globe Artichoke

Pink
Cumin
Soapwort
Centaury
Gravel Root
Pink Hyssop
Coriander

Companion Planting

Though Companion Planting has not yet been scientifically proven, a great deal of research is being done to confirm what most gardeners already know.

Plants exude chemicals or "phytotoxins" as they are sometimes referred to, which can inhibit the growth or development of other plants near them. This phenomenon is called allelopathy. Just as some plants should not be placed near one another, other plants benefit by being neighbors to enhance their health or growth. Plants impact each other either by inhibiting growth or enhancing growth, repelling, trapping or attracting certain insects or pests.

This is what we call companion planting; placing plants near to one another so that each will benefit from the other. Herbs with deep root systems hold water better than those with shallow roots which dry out in the heat of summer. Therefore, planting them together creates a small eco-system of survival. Large leafy plants can give protection from sun or wind to smaller shade-lovers. Flowering herbs can attract beneficial insects and aid with the pollination of their neighbors. Herbs, fruits, flowers and vegetables can all benefit from companion planting.

The companion planting chart on the following page will help you decide which of your plants should be neighbors so they may be productive and thriving garden community members!

Pests	Plants that Repel Pests
Ants	pennyroyal, peppermint, spearmint, wormwood, tansy
Aphids	scented herbs like chives, catnip, eucalyptus, fennel, coriander, garlic, mustard, mint, nasturtiums, marigolds
Asparagus Beetle	tomato, basil, parsley
Blackfly	nettle, mint
Cabbage Butterfly	southernwood
Cabbage Looper	pennyroyal, southernwood, wormwood, thyme, sage, spearmint, peppermint, dill, garlic, hyssop, onion, nasturtiums, eucalyptus
Cabbage Maggot	wormwood, sage, marigolds, radish, garlic, mint
Carrot Fly	rosemary, sage, wormwood, onion, lettuce, leek

Pests	Plants that Repel Pests
Codling Moth	wormwood, garlic
Colorado Potato Beetle	tansy, eucalyptus, onion, coriander, catnip, nasturtiums
Corn Earworm	geranium, marigolds, cosmos
Cucumber Beetle	radish, rue, catnip, marigolds, nasturtiums
Cutworm	spiny amaranth
Flea Beetle	peppermint, spearmint, catnip, rue, southernwood, wormwood, tansy
Japanese Beetle	garlic, chives, tansy, catnip
Leafhopper	petunias, geraniums
Mexican Bean Beetle	rosemary, marigolds
Mole	narcissus, castor beans

Pests	Plants that Repel Pests
Mouse	wormwood
Peach Borer	garlic
Rabbit	onion, garlic, marigolds
Slugs, Snails	garlic, fennel, rosemary
Spider Mite	coriander
Squash Bug	peppermint, spearmint, nasturtiums, catnip, petunias, radish, tansy
Squash Vine Borer	radish
Tomato Hornworm	opal basil, dill, borage
Whitefly	peppermint, wormwood, thyme, nasturtiums

Beneficial Insects	Plants that Attract Beneficial Insects
Bees (pollinators)	Coriander, summer savory, Queen Anne's lace, dill, anise, borage, fennel, yarrow
Butterflies (pollinators)	Plants in the carrot, mustard, mint, daisy families
Spiders (eat insects)	Thyme, rosemary, any low-growth, dense plants
Lady Bugs (eat Aphids)	Chamomile, thyme, savory
Wasps (Braconid, Icheumonid, Chalcid varieties) (eat insects)	Yarrow, wild carrot, fennel, mustard, Queen Anne's lace, evergreens

Also:

Prevent Scab, Blackspot	Chives
Improve soil	Flax, clover, buckwheat
Improve crop yield	Borage, hyssop, chamomile
Improve flavor	Coriander

Being informed about which plants make good companions is just as important as knowing which plants should keep away from one another. The following is another useful chart to ensure greater success in the garden.

Herb	Companion Plant	Keep Away
anise	coriander	carrot
basil	tomatoes, peppers	------
bee balm	tomatoes	------
borage	tomatoes, beans, strawberries	------
chamomile	cucumber, onion, most herbs	------
chervil	radish	------
chives	tomatoes, carrots, grapes, roses	beans, peas
coriander	anise	fennel

Herb	Companion Plant	Keep Away
dandelion	fruit trees	------
dill	lettuce, cabbage	tomatoes, carrots, onion
fennel	------	beans, peppers
garlic	roses	beans, peas
horseradish	potatoes	------
hyssop	cabbage, grapes	------
larkspur	cabbage, beans	beets
lovage	beans	------
marigold	tomatoes, roses, potatoes	------
mint	tomatoes, cabbage	------
nettle	potatoes	------

Herb	Companion Plant	Keep Away
onion	cabbage, lettuce, beets, strawberries	sage, beans, peas
oregano	beans	------
rosemary	beans	------
rue	figs	cabbage, basil, sage
sage	tomatoes, marjoram, cabbage, carrots, strawberries	onion
tansy	blackberries, raspberries, roses	collards
tarragon	most vegetables	------
thyme	tomatoes, potatoes, eggplant	------
wormwood	------	most vegetables
yarrow	most aromatic herbs	------

Lori Trojan

Care & Maintenance of the Herb Garden

One of the true beauties of growing herbs is the minimal maintenance they require. Unlike flowers, fruit trees or vegetables which require daily maintenance of some kind, herbs are more characteristic of weeds and need little fuss.

Weeding

One of the most productive things you can do regularly to improve your herb garden is to remove unwanted weeds. Be cautious as tiny seedlings that may appear near a flourishing plant may be new shoots attempting to spread. Do not remove these thinking they are weeds! If unsure, let them grow a little larger until you can identify them. Once you are sure you have identified a weed, pluck it out by the roots and remove it. Never use an inorganic weed killer. The best method is to pull them out by hand or rake with a hoe.

Pesky Pests

Companion planting often keeps pest problems to a minimum as some herbs act as insect repellents to others. Even though herbs tend to be relatively pest and disease free if grown under the right conditions, it is advisable to take organic measures to expel pesky insects and to rid plants of disease if necessary. There are many choices of effective commercial organic formulas for pest and disease control on the market today. One of the best organic measures available is neem oil, found in your local hardware store. Diatomaceous earth, pyrethrin and releasing beneficial insects like lady bugs and praying mantis can also be effective. A word of warning about praying mantis. They will eat pesky insects but will also eat butterflies, bees and hummingbirds so keep them away from pollinator gardens. There are also many recipes for making home-made brews which are equally effective. I recommend the book by Jerry Baker called, *Giant Book of Garden Solutions*. This informative and humorous text gives useful organic recipes and advice for treating and feeding plants of all types, including herbs.

Pruning

Cutting back herbs in spring and/or fall is always recommended as in so doing, a vast supply of fresh new foliage will grow back. Some herbs may be allowed to flower for aromatherapy, culinary or medicinal purposes. However if you do not have a specific use for the flowers, cut back before flowering to increase the overall size of the plant. For example, lavender should be cut back in early fall to remove flower heads and keep bushes tight for over-wintering.

In spring, cut back about 1-inch from the previous year's growth, making sure some green foliage remains around the bottom. This will ensure a bushy spurt of growth for the new season. Every time you prune an herb to use it for a desired purpose, it will grow back faster and thicker. Much the same as your own hair; the more often you trim it, the faster and thicker it will grow!

Deadheading

Like any flowering plants, deadheading is recommended in order to stimulate new growth. Allow your plants to direct their energy into establishing roots and producing new growth instead of supporting dead or dying stems and flower heads. Collect seeds from deadheads to plant later or let seeds drop to allow self-seeding if you don't mind where the plants spread. Herbs are also very easy to transplant so allowing them to self-seed is an easy way to encourage new growth. You can move the young shoots later when the time is right.

Before winter, turn all dead plant matter back into the soil as this will bring up minerals from the subsoil as they decay. Tilling them back into the Earth will help to enrich the soil for the next planting season.

Mulching

Herbs do not require mulching and in some cases, too much moisture retention can rot the plant. Mulch only those herbs that love moisture such as Bee Balm and those from the mint family. Depending on the climate (zone) in which you live, most herbs will over-winter well though they will remain in a dormant state until spring. Cutting back herbs in fall to prepare for over-wintering is a good idea but to what extent lies solely with you. Leaving dead foliage on the plants at the end of fall can sometimes help to protect them from the cold and wind, in which case dead foliage can be trimmed back at the first signs of spring. Letting dry dead leaves accumulate around your plants can also help to protect them from the cold however with ground covers such as thyme, dead leaves can encourage fungus due to mold and damp.

Container Gardens

Growing herbs in pots or containers is relatively maintenance free except for the need to water on a regular basis. Soil in containers tends to dry out quickly and the plants depend on you for feeding and watering. Nutrients in potting soil can be usurped from year to year. Therefore, a liquid feed is recommended every 2 weeks during the growing season. Consider changing out all or part of the soil in your pots each year and start with a good feed in early spring.

Be aware that if your plants are happy and growing rapidly, they can outgrow the container in which they began. If roots are growing out of the bottom of the pot, if soil is becoming dry quickly or new growth has slowed, these are signs that your herb has become "potbound" and requires re-planting into a larger container. Herbs may die of "suffocation" if they do not have enough room to expand. If you cannot repot or the container holds several herbs with intertwined roots and it is too difficult to repot without damaging the plants, remove about 2 inches of the soil from the top of the pot and replace with new potting soil. Give a good feed with compost or a slow-release fertilizer and don't feed again for about 1 month. You should then start to see new growth begin again.

If your winters are very cold, try to bring potted herbs indoors to the house or the garage. It is possible to repot from the garden and transplant outdoor plants indoors before winter strikes. Simply choose a dry, preferably cloudy day and dig a clump of herbs from out of the ground (gently, making sure to leave roots intact). Dig deep and separate the clump from the remainder of the plant so that the portion left in the ground remains healthy and undisturbed. Plant the unearthed clump into pots and water well, being sure that you have chosen pots the appropriate size to encourage growth and to accommodate the mature roots. Cut back the top growth by about 1-2 inches and place pots in a brightly lit area. Leave a light on during daylight hours and shut the light off at night to simulate nature. Harvest regularly to promote new growth. In spring, return containers to the outdoors or replant into the garden after the last frost has passed. If it is not possible to bring herb pots indoors, consider burying them up to the rim in the soil as this will act as insulation from the cold.

Gardening is about experimentation combined with trial and error. The best way to learn about care and maintenance is to keep a few of these tips in mind and watch. Note your plants' behaviors in every season of the year. With every passing month, you will become more of an expert on those herbs that you are growing. Each time you add a new one, you have the opportunity to watch and learn.

Before you know it, you will be an expert on every herb you have nurtured. Caution: Herb gardening can be addictive!

Lori Trojan

Perennials, Annuals & Growing from Seed

The most simple, efficient and inexpensive way to grow herbs is by propagating seeds. This will allow you to grow a large number of plants on a budget. Annuals, biennials and perennials may be grown from seed. Cuttings may be used to propagate perennials, as well as shrubs and trees. Seeds may be grown in containers or directly into the ground, even into the cracks between paving stones if you wish!

Annuals and Biennials

Sowing herb seeds can be done at different times of the year. For example, in spring hardy annuals like marigolds and borage can be sown, providing flowers in fall or the following spring. In late summer or early fall, sow biennials like caraway and angelica for flowers the following summer. Some herbs which have short lives like parsley, chervil or coriander can be sown every three to four weeks throughout spring and fall. By doing this, you will have a constant supply of fresh herbs all through the growing season. Some herbs are more difficult to grow from seed like basil as they need to be kept constantly warm and moist. However, they can be sown indoors in late spring and kept at a minimum temperature of 70°F. If you are in a warm climate, basil may be sown directly outdoors. If starting seedlings indoors, do not plant out until all threats of frost have passed. Always thin out seedlings twice; once soon after germination and again after about two to three weeks so that only the strongest are left to survive.

Perennials

Perennial herbs may be grown from seed sown directly into the ground or into containers in the warmth of spring. However, the easiest way to grow perennials is from taking cuttings or dividing already established plants. Mound layering is also an easy way to grow new herb plants without sowing seeds. This method works for woody shrub herbs like rosemary, sage, lavender, hyssop and thyme. In spring, mound up soil over the woody base of the plant, leaving just the green tops exposed. This will actually stimulate new growth and shoots will appear in the mounded soil. Cut off these shoots from the mother plants and replant them elsewhere.

Many perennials are grown from bulbous roots in which case you must wait until fall when the plant has died down and all the nutrients have returned to the bulb. Then, gently dig up bulbs and transplant as in the case of lily of the valley.

Sowing Seeds Indoors

To sow seeds indoors, line the bottom of prepared flats with paper towels (1 sheet thick) and add a layer of perlite or fish tank gravel over the towel. Next, add a growing medium. 1 part potting soil, 2 parts sand or vermiculite and 1 part peat moss is the recommended soil mix. Level this and firm gently on the flat. Plant seeds in rows about 2" apart. For finer seeds, you can mix the seed with sand and it becomes easier to sow. Put a thin layer of sand or fine soil over the top of the seeds. For angelica, chamomile, dill, chervil, lemon balm, feverfew, yarrow, savories or mugwort, do not cover with sand or soil as these seeds need light to germinate.

Always label the flats and record the date of sowing. Mist the flats gently with water and cover with plastic, glass or damp newspapers and put them in a constant temperature of 65-70° F. Start seedlings 6-8 weeks before you plan to transfer them outdoors. Keep in mind, some perennials take 4-8 weeks just to germinate, so check seed packets or ask before sowing.

Once the first seedlings appear, remove the cover from your flats and move them to a sunny spot or under fluorescent lights. They will need 12-15 hours of light daily. If your light does not come from an overhead source, be sure to turn the flats so each new growth gets equal time in the sun! At this time, snip out any seedlings that are crowding the rows - do not pull out as they may disturb the roots of the seedlings that you want to survive.

Keep soil moist, not soaked and when the seedlings are about 2" tall, thin again so that the strongest plants will survive. At this point, it is time to "harden off" your seedlings.

After the threat of frost has passed, start by putting your flats outdoors in a safe place in the sun for an hour or so and return them inside. Continue to increase the outdoor time each day until after about 10 days, they should be able to withstand the outdoor environment all day.

When you are ready to transplant your seedlings into the

garden, cut them from the flat with about 1-2" of soil around them in a square and transplant them, soil and all. Do not try to pick them up from the root to transplant as they will not be strong enough to withstand this.

Harvesting Seeds

Ideally, you will be able to harvest seeds from your own garden as well as purchasing new seeds from an organic source. Once a flower is fertilized, a seed starts to develop. When flower petals have finished their job of attracting pollinating insects, they will wither and fall off the plant to reveal the seed below. As the seed continues to develop, it dries and turns brown, feeling dry to the touch. At this stage the seeds are ready to harvest. Not all herbs produce seeds and therefore, sometimes it is easier to purchase plants such as tarragon, mint, some thymes and some sages. These can be grown from cuttings, divided or mound layered to propagate as well.

Self-Seeding

One of the most natural occurrences in the garden is the process of self-seeding. If you do not harvest the seeds or dead-head the flowers after they wilt, the herb plants will naturally drop their seeds onto the ground. Some herbs like lady's mantle, caraway, motherwort, marigold and elecampane will self-seed prolifically. If conditions are favorable, you can just sit back and watch the new growth with very little involvement. You can always transplant these seedlings later to a more desirable place. Sometimes as a bonus, this self-seeding can cause an interesting hybrid to appear.

Animals and birds will also be your garden helpers in harvesting and distributing seeds. Seeds in fruits specifically will be eaten by these creatures, go through their digestive tracts and be dropped into the soil by way of their waste materials.

Also herb seeds from cleavers, agrimony and burdock will attach themselves to anything that brushes up against them and will drop in various other locations. Some seeds will be blown by the wind to far locations and others will drop without germinating perhaps for years, waiting for the perfect conditions.

Some plants have a natural "catapulting" mechanism which will throw the seed some distance to assure propagation of the species. Some seeds can survive being under water for long periods and may be washed in and out with the ocean tide, only to germinate months later in a distant location.

Harvesting, Drying & Freezing Herbs

Gathering or harvesting herbs at the right time of the season, in the right weather and at the right time of day will make all the difference in determining the flavor, scent and usefulness of each particular herb. The level of essential oil fluctuates with temperature and light, therefore timing is everything when gathering for medicinal purposes. If you are harvesting for culinary purposes only, the timing is not as important and can be done on an as-needed basis.

Harvesting

Basic tips for harvesting herbs for medicinal purposes:

- Gather on a warm dry day just after the dew has evaporated but before the sun becomes very hot in the afternoon. The heat will greatly reduce the vital essential oil in the plant.
- Try to keep the plant's shape intact and encourage new growth after harvesting by choosing shoots from the outer growth of the plant.
- Use foliage free from damage and insects.
- Generally, gather buds before fully opened into flowers

- Flowers can be harvested at the same time of day as leaves. Make sure to shake flower heads or buds to allow any insects to drop off. If open flower heads are required, pick immediately after opening. Leaves and shoots are best before flowers have opened. Handle leaves gently as volatile essential oils will be released if they are bruised by rough handling.
- Harvest roots at the end of the growing season-usually in late fall when the maximum amount of nutrients have been restored to the roots. Brush or wash soil gently from roots before using but do not soak in water. Dry as much as possible after washing.
- Collecting seeds should be done in late summer or early fall by removing whole seedheads after they have turned brown but have not fully ripened enough to release seeds.

Preserving

There are several methods of preserving herbs; storing, drying by air and by microwave, freezing, and preserving in liquid such as vinegar or oil.

Storing:

Store dried herbs by chopping or breaking into pieces and place in dark ceramic or glass containers as light will deteriorate them. **DO NOT WASH THE HERBS BEFORE STORING OR DRYING.** This will encourage mold and will ruin the plant.

Drying:

Cut and tie stems together. Hang upside down in a well-ventilated, warm, dry place away from direct light. A closet, shed or attic might do well for this process. Keep hanging bunches away from walls. Temperatures in your chosen drying area should be about 90-93°F. After 2-3 days, the temperature should be reduced to about 77-80°F. to complete the drying process. Another option is to scatter leaves, flowers, and stems on a flat tray in one layer on paper towels. Leaving them in a warm dry place will cause them to get crispy-dry. You may choose to use the microwave to dry herbs by placing them in a single layer on paper towels and microwaving them on 50% power for 2-3 minutes, checking every 30 seconds. You may have to rearrange them to allow for even drying. Cool the herbs, crumble and store. To dry seedheads, place them in a brown paper bag or hang them upside down wrapped in muslin to catch the seeds as they are released. Place them in a warm dry place during this process and after all the seeds have fallen, remove them and store in jars or bags. Seeds to be used for sowing should be kept in a cool dry place, kept frost-free and must be labeled and dated. To dry roots and barks, remove excess soil then peel, chop or slice them before laying out on a baking pan to dry. Ideally, they should be dried in an oven at 120-150°F. or dried in a dehydrator until brittle.

Rule of thumb for drying times is generally as follows:
- When the herb crumbles between your fingers, it is ready to be stored.
- If leaves are dry before the stems, strip the leaves and store while continuing to dry the stems.
- Stems should break or snap when dry. If they bend, they are not fully dry.
- Flower petals should not crumble but should still be slightly pliable.
- Barks and roots should be dry enough to snap.

Freezing:

Several herb varieties do better by freezing rather than drying to preserve. Parsley and basil are two such herbs. Just put whole sprigs into plastic bags or air-tight containers into the freezer, label and use as desired. Another way to freeze efficiently is to break fresh herbs into ice cube trays, fill with water and make herbal ice cubes. They are beautiful and can be melted individually by placing in a sieve or dropped into a culinary concoction as is. Freezing mint in this way is a lovely enhancement to summer iced teas.

Herbal Oils and Vinegars:

Preserving in these mediums can enhance herbal flavors and makes them easily usable in salad dressings, sauces, soups, stews, casseroles, etc. Herbs such as rosemary, thyme, oregano, tarragon and lavender are a few that do well preserved in this way. To make an oil or vinegar, fill a glass jar or container with fresh herb and then fill to the top with either oil (use sunflower, olive, almond or other oil desired) or warmed vinegar (wine, apple cider or champagne work well). Please see specific instructions for preserving herbs in oils or vinegars in the following chapter. When using vinegar, crush the herb slightly to release flavors. Put a tight-fitting lid on the container. Metal lids will often rust when using vinegar, so try placing waxed paper between the lid and jar. Leave the bottle in the sun for about 2 weeks, shaking gently each day. After 2 weeks, strain herbs from the oil or vinegar and add a fresh few sprigs if desired before storing in a cool dark place.

Tinctures, Teas, Infusions, Decoctions, Syrups, Salves, Oils & Vinegars

Whether using your harvested herbs for culinary or medicinal purposes, a variety of preparation methods are detailed below along with a few recipes to inspire you. You will be surprised at how easy it is to make these in your own kitchen.

Tinctures

Tinctures are a concentrated format in which to take herbal medicines. Tinctures are herbs infused into alcohol (usually vodka or brandy), vinegar or glycerin for internal use and into rubbing alcohol for external use. The liquid base used to infuse or extract the herbs is called the menstruum.

They are safe, highly effective and will maintain their potency and shelf life for many years. They are also fast-acting and though I recommend ingesting them mixed into a little water or fruit juice, they may be taken undiluted sublingually (under the tongue) for even faster results. Tinctures can also be diluted in water for mouthwashes, baths, soaks and fomentations. They can be mixed into a base to make suppositories as well.

To make a tincture, you will need:
- A quantity of fresh herb or the plant of your choice to be tinctured
- 100 proof Vodka or organic grain alcohol (vinegar or glycerin may be substituted*)
- Glass jar with tight-fitting lid
- Labels
- (optional) 1 oz. bottle with dropper top

*A vinegar tincture will not last as long and may not be as potent as an alcohol preparation. However, vinegars do a beautiful job of extracting minerals, alkaloids and vitamins from your plant material. Vinegar also has its own healing properties, so this can provide a double-duty healing effect. Just 1 Tablespoon of these vinegars on a salad for example, adds a huge flavor enhancement as well as an additional nutrient source. Use vinegars at room temperature. I recommend using organic apple cider vinegar or wine vinegar. Do not use white distilled vinegar as this is a product made from a chemical extraction process and is not ideal for consumption. (However, this vinegar is great for cleaning windows!)

Though glycerin is a menstruum that may be used instead of alcohol or vinegar, it is not as effective at the extraction process. Glycerin is a good base for those that have an aversion to alcohol or vinegar and for children who prefer the sweet taste. Glycerin is a mucilaginous, sweet liquid which can be made from animal fat, so be sure to purchase 100% vegetable glycerin. Dilute the glycerin with equal parts water and use in the same method as alcohol or vinegar when preparing the tincture of choice.

Follow this simple method:

- Identify the herb or plant you wish to tincture and pick those parts recommended (root, leaves, stems, flowers, etc.) at optimum harvest time, disposing of any damaged parts.
- You do not need to wash or rinse the plant unless you are tincturing a root and must remove heavy soil.
- Tear or chop the herb/plant into small pieces. Place into the glass jar you have chosen (any size from a baby food jar to a canning jar or larger).
- Fill the jar to the top with the plant material but do not compact for all but roots. If using roots, fill the jar ¼ full.
- Pour alcohol to the top rim of the jar. Use a wooden chop stick or similar to gently press plant material down without compacting to eliminate air bubbles.
- Screw lid on tightly.

- Label the jar with the name of the herb or plant used, the part (flower, leaf, root, etc.), type of liquid (alcohol, vinegar or glycerin), and the date. Within 24-48 hours, top off the jar if necessary with additional liquid if the tincture has settled.
- Store in a dark place.

After 6 weeks, use a turkey baster to transfer liquid into a 1 oz. dark glass bottle with a dropper top. Be sure to label this bottle with the same information as the original and keep safely away from children.

Dosage for a vinegar tincture:
- 1 teaspoon or 15ml. per 100lbs. or 50 kilograms of body weight.

Dosage for an alcohol tincture:
- One dropper-full unless otherwise stated.
- Dosages are by experience and experimentation. Start with small amounts and increase dosage until the desired effect is achieved.
- Start with 5-10 drops daily and increase to dropperfuls as needed.

Teas, Infusions, Decoctions and Syrups

Teas, infusions, decoctions and syrups are considered to be water-based medicines and are very effective for certain types of herb usage. Herbs that are high in volatile oils are best prepared as teas rather than infusions. They usually taste good and are comforting as well as healing. Herbs that make effective teas are chamomile, fennel seeds, anise, and fenugreek, to name a scant few. Dried herbs make the best preparation as the boiling water breaks down plant cell walls more efficiently than using a fresh herb. Nutrients are then released when rehydrating. Teas are also more potent using dried rather than fresh plant material.

Teas

A tea is described as a nourishing, comforting drink made by a brief infusion of a plant in hot water. After water, it is the most widely consumed drink in the world. Gather dried organic plant material of choice. Use approximately 1 teaspoon (minimum) of herb per cup of water. Pour boiling water over herb material in a pot with tight fitting lid. Stir and cover. Allow to steep for about 10 minutes. Strain into a cup and enjoy.

Infusions

An Infusion is a water-based method used primarily for preparing nourishing herbs such as nettle, dandelion, red clover, oatstraw, lemon balm, borage and burdock to name a few. A larger amount of dried herb is used and the steep time is much longer than in tea preparations. Infusions may be sipped like tea or used as bath soaks, compresses, fomentations and poultices. Typically, the dosage for an Infusion is 2-4 cups daily, though the dose also depends on the herb used. Halve the dosage for a child or weak person. Seek advice before administering to an infant.

Leaves:

Use 1-2 very large handfuls of dried leaves per quart of water. Place dried herbs into a ceramic or stainless steel soup pot (or glass canning jar) and pour boiling water over the top. Stir thoroughly and cover with a tight-fitting lid. Allow the infusion to steep for a minimum of 4 hours. Steep time can extend up to 10 hours. Strain the herb as you pour the infusion into a pitcher. Compost the herb or save it to use as a poultice or compress.

Flowers:

Use approximately 1 ounce of dried flowers to one quart of water and follow the directions above for leaves, reducing steep time to 2 hours. If combining flowers and leaves, steep time may be up to 4 hours.

Roots:

Use 1 ounce of dried chopped root to 1 pint of water. Follow directions for leaves and steep for 8-12 hours.

Barks:

Usually, the directions above for roots also applies to barks with a few exceptions. For example, slippery elm bark only requires 1 hour of steep time. Wild cherry, willow and oak bark require 6-8 hours of steep time.

Seeds:

Making seed infusions is a little more rare. However because seeds release their medicinal properties into water quickly, steep time should not generally exceed 10-30 minutes. Use 1 ounce of dried seed to 1 pint of water and follow same directions above for leaves.

Decoctions

Decoctions are a more concentrated form of an infusion. They are prepared in the very same manner however decoctions are reduced by half through evaporation creating a more potent preparation. Because of the greater potency, reduce the dosage to a quarter of that of an infusion. Fill a stainless steel or ceramic pan with 1 pint of prepared infusion and heat very gently, just enough to create an evaporating steam without bringing the liquid to a boil. When the liquid infusion is reduced by half, remove the pan from the heat. This is a slow process and must be watched carefully to avoid boiling.

Syrups

From a decoction, a syrup is created.

Method for making a syrup:

For each cup of decoction, add 4 ounces of fresh raw honey, heating just enough to melt it into the liquid. 1 Tablespoon of alcohol may be added to preserve and enhance the natural medicinal qualities of the syrup. Generally, dosage is 1 teaspoon as needed.

Salves

Salves are relatively easy to make and require an infused oil to be used as a base. The other vital ingredient is beeswax which carries its own unique healing properties. Beeswax acts as a carrier for the oil and allows it to be more easily absorbed into the skin.

For every one cup of infused oil, add ¼ cup pure shredded beeswax. Gently heat the ingredients (using a glass coffee pot on the stove top works well for this process) over a low heat, stirring continuously until the mixture has melted completely. You may add a few drops of essential oil to a salve before pouring into a glass jar. Allow to cool.

If the salve is too loose, reheat and add more beeswax. If the cooled salve is too thick, reheat and add more oil until the desired consistency is attained. Cover with a tight-fitting lid when completely cooled to avoid condensation, causing mold to form. Apply salve topically.

One of my favorite salve recipes:
- Equal parts comfrey oil, yarrow oil and St. John's Wort oil combined to make 4 ounces of infused oil.
- 4-8 drops of lavender essential oil
- 1 ounce shredded beeswax

Infused Oils

Infused oils are easy to prepare but should not be confused with essential oils which are very difficult to make as essential oils require distilling equipment and a complex process for extraction. Essential oils must not be ingested and must be used in small dosages as they can be toxic. Essential oils are used in aromatherapy, perfumes and scented products as well as medicinals. Infused oils are very safe and used in massage oils, bath and body care products, salves and are delicious in salads as a dressing. There are a variety of recommended oils which can be used as a base. A lighter organic oil makes the best product. Olive oil keeps the longest and has many healing properties of its own. Sweet almond oil, apricot kernel oil, grapeseed oil and nut oils are all good choices for making infused oils.

To make an infused oil you will need:
- A very dry dark glass bottle or jar (leave in a warm place prior to preparation to make sure the inside is completely dry).
- Oil of choice
- Quantity of fresh herb material, chopped coarsely
- A few drops of Vitamin E oil (if desired for preserving)

One of the greatest challenges in making an infused oil is to prevent mold from forming. Be absolutely sure that the jar you have chosen to use is bone dry and the chopped herb material is also very dry. Do not gather herbs until they have been at least 3 days in the sun with no rain. Gather after the morning dew has evaporated completely, preferably later in the afternoon.

Making an Infused Oil:
- Fill the jar loosely with the herb material of choice and slowly pour the oil over the herb to the rim of the jar. Stir with a wooden chopstick to release air bubbles and evenly distribute the plant material. Cover the jar with a tight-fitting lid and label. Place in a cool dark area for 6 weeks before using, gently turning the jar over and over once each day.
- If mold has grown throughout the infusion after 6 weeks, discard and start again. It is wise to keep jars of oil on a tray as they infuse. Some herbs release gas bubbles, causing the oil to leak from the lid creating a messy clean-up.

- After 6 weeks, strain the oil into another glass jar and discard the plant material. Leave the fresh jar of oil overnight and check the next day for any oil/water separation. If you notice this, just slowly pour off the oil into another jar and dispose of the water left on the bottom.
- You may wish to add a Vitamin E capsule (prick the capsule and pour out the oil) or add a few drops of liquid Vitamin E to the infused oil as this helps to avoid rancidity. Healing infused oils may be used topically for skin conditions, abrasions, wounds, burns, rashes, cracked or dry skin. They make a wonderful healing massage oil and are soothing when added to a bath. Infused oils are a necessary ingredient in salves and healing lotions, creams and butters.
- Flavored infused oils make delicious sauces and salad dressings.

Infused Vinegars

Making an infused vinegar is similar to making an infused oil. When making an infused vinegar, warm the vinegar over a very low heat until just slightly over room temperature. Wine, apple cider or champagne vinegars work well. Pour into a wide mouth glass jar. Crush your herb of choice slightly to release flavors before adding to the liquid. Place a tight-fitting lid on the container. Metal lids will often rust when using vinegar, so try placing waxed paper between the lid and jar. Leave the bottle in the sun for about 2 weeks, shaking gently each day. After 2 weeks, strain the herbs from the vinegar and add a fresh few sprigs if desired before storing in a cool dark place. Flavored vinegars make delicious salad dressings and can be used for a variety of other purposes. If using apple cider vinegar, taking a Tablespoon by mouth each day is advised to ward off the common cold.

Decorating with Herbs

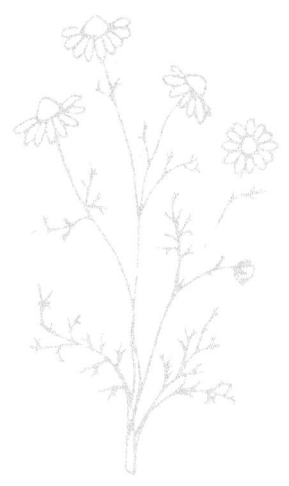

There is another side of herbs besides the medicinal, aromatherapy and culinary aspects. How could we possibly overlook the simple beauty and exquisite aromatic qualities of these wild plants? Following are some creative ideas for using herbs everyday to decorate your life.

Potpourri

Making a potpourri involves the use of dried herbs and plant materials. By far the best materials to use for a fragrant and beautiful potpourri include unique whole leaves and flowers, spices (cinnamon sticks, cloves, vanilla pods, fennel seeds, juniper berries, etc.), dried citrus peel (trim peel from fruit and place on a baking tray in a low oven temperature for 10 minutes to dry. Check frequently), cedar bark, sandalwood bark, frankincense and myrrh to name a few.

Once the herbs you have chosen for your potpourri have completed the drying process, layer the ingredients separately in glass jars with tight-fitting lids. Layers should be about 2 cm. deep. Always keep each type of plant material in separate containers so that many combinations can be mixed as you desire. Sprinkle each layer evenly with $\frac{1}{2}$ teaspoon coarse salt and $\frac{1}{2}$ teaspoon orris root powder to preserve color and maintain a fresh appearance. Once the lids are in place, label each jar and store in a dark cool area for 3 weeks.

After 3 weeks, assemble the jars and any other materials you wish to add to your personal pot-pourri. Pour the contents of each into an open decorative bowl and stir. A few drops of essential oil may be added for more fragrance.

After a time when the scent is gone, put the whole mixture into a sealed plastic bag with a few drops of essential oil, shake and store for up to 2 weeks. Replace in the decorative bowl for a refreshed scent.

Floral Potpourri

- 4 Tablespoons rose petals
- 4 Tablespoons lavender flowers (with or without stems)
- 4 Tablespoons chamomile flowers
- 2 Tablespoons marigold petals
- 4-6 echinacea flower heads
- 2 Tablespoons salt
- 2 Tablespoons orris root powder
- 6-8 drops lavender essential oil
- Prepare using method above.

Herbal Potpourri

- 8 Tablespoons dried mint leaves
- 6 Tablespoons dried rosemary leaves
- 2 Tablespoons dried sage leaves
- 2 Tablespoons dried thyme leaves with stems
- 2 Tablespoons dried oregano leaves
- 4 Tablespoons dried lemon balm leaves
- 2 Tablespoons salt
- 2 Tablespoons orris root powder
- 6-8 drops oregano or rosemary essential oil
- Prepare using method for Floral Potpourri.

Sachets and Scent Pillows

Sachets and scent pillows are neither difficult nor time-consuming to make and produce inexpensive and fragrant gifts. Potpourri can be used in a scent pillow as well as loose dried herbs and flowers.

Quick Stitch Sachet

- Gather remnants of fabric at your local fabric shop measuring approximately 8 x 11 inches. Choose any small patterns or solid colors in lightweight cotton, linen or silk.
- Fold the measured remnant and cut fabric pieces in half lengthwise, right sides together, and stitch with a machine or by hand down the long open side and one short side, using a $\frac{1}{2}$" seam allowance.
- Fold the top of the bag about halfway down over the bag itself and press with a warm iron. This piece will be tucked into the bag when turned right-side out.
- Turn the bag right-side out and fill 2/3 full with dried scented mixture.
- Tie with a 1/4" wide ribbon measuring about 18" in length, making a double knot to secure and finishing with a tidy bow.

Handkerchief Magic

Using a warm iron, press a unique lace or linen handkerchief. Lay flat on an even surface and place dried scented herb or potpourri into the center. Draw up the edges with a satin ribbon. Magic: instant scent sachet!

Bath Soak Scent Pillow

Follow the stitching method for the Quick Stitch Sachet using muslin or fine mesh fabric measuring 8 x 6 inches and secure with twine instead of ribbon. Drop the sachet into a warm bath for a soothing fragrant soak. Bath Soak Scent Pillows can be used 3-4 times, allowing the pillow to dry between baths. Try this heavenly filler combination:

Equal parts rose petals, lavender flowers, chamomile flowers, rolled whole oats, dried lemon or orange peel, 2 rosemary sprigs.

Bouquets and Floral Arrangements

Bouquets and floral arrangements do not have to be from fresh flowers. The dried variety make a beautiful presentation and with care, last forever. The scent can be refreshed time and again.

Tussie-Mussies

Such a wonderful name for a small nosegay of scented dried flowers! Tussie-Mussies have a fascinating history dating back to the 17th century when they were given for medicinal purposes, for air fresheners, as covers for more unpleasant scents, as gifts and as tokens of love.

Gather the following materials:
- Two 6" paper lace doilies
- ¼" wide, self-adhesive floral tape
- ¼" wide decorative ribbon
- Dried green stems with leaves (try lamb's ears, artemisia, silver lace)
- 1 rose for the center
- 6 additional flowers with stems
- Super glue

- Fold one doily into halves, then quarters, then in half again, creating a fluted effect. Cut a hole in the center of the doily.
- Slip 3-4 greenery stems through the hole and trim bottoms so they come to a point.
- From the base of the doily, wrap stems with floral tape. Stand upright in a cup or glass.
- Apply a small amount of glue to the base of the rose and place in the center. Press firmly to secure.
- Apply glue in the same manner as in step 4 to other flowers with stems and arrange around the rose, pressing each firmly to secure.
- Flute the second doily as you did the first, cutting a hole through the center and slip the stems of the tussie-mussie through.
- Wrap ribbon around the stems at the base of the doilies to secure the bunch, double knot and finish with a tidy bow.
- A few drops of essential oil may be added.

Herbal Arrangements

Gather the following materials:
- Floral foam block, knife, container, assorted dried greens, herbs, grasses or dried flowers of your choice with wired stems.
- Cut a piece of floral foam so that it fits into a container of your choosing with 2" above the rim. Using a knife, trim the foam so that it is rounded at the corners.
- Starting at the top then continuing to work down the sides, insert greenery into the foam block. Stems should be inserted to their halfway point to remain secure.
- Insert the wire-stemmed herbs/flowers in varying heights, larger ones inserted into the bottom and smaller ones at top.
- Apply drops of essential oil if desired.

Wreaths

There are several different types of wreaths: floral, herbal, candle wreaths, garlands and wearable wreaths for hats or wedding veils, to name a few.

Herb Wreath

Gather the following materials:

- A straw wreath form (finished wreath will be 2-4 inches larger than the form), florist pins, sprigs of 4-5 dried herb varieties 5" long, (try using artemisia, parsley, sage, silver leaf, lamb's ears, lavender, rosemary, tansy, etc.) wire loop to hang the wreath.
- Starting with the lightest color herb, arrange several sprigs stems outward, creating a curved row on the form. Attach the sprigs with florist pins to secure.
- Make a second and third row with the same herb so that you have three rows equal in distance apart.
- Keep all rows in place with pins, keeping all sprigs curving in the same direction and overlapping to hide the pins. Alongside each row made of the first herb, use the same technique to make three rows of the next one and continue until all herbs are incorporated, adding darkest color last. There should be 12 rows when completed.
- Attach the wire loop to the back for hanging.

Floral Waters

Floral waters are a fresh way to add scent into your home and though old-fashioned, this is their charm! Floral infused water can be used for room sprays, bath splashes, steam ironing and scenting sheets among other things.

Lavender Water

- 16 oz. distilled water
- 2 oz. vodka or organic grain alcohol
- 2 Tablespoons lavender flowers
- 8 drops lavender essential oil
- Spray bottle or glass jar

Method:
Be sure the bottle or jar you are using is very clean. Add alcohol to the bottle. Mix in flowers so they are completely wet. Add the essential oil. Store in a cool dark place. After 1 week, strain the flowers if desired, add the distilled water and the floral water is ready to use. Chamomile, rose flowers or any other fragrant herb or flower of your choosing may be substituted for lavender flowers. Essential oil scents may be interchanged as well.

Lori Trojan

Guide to Growing Herbs

Frequently Asked Questions

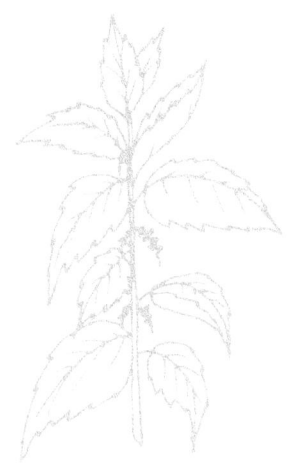

Are extracts made from fresh herbs better than those made from dried herbs?

Often a fresh herb tincture is better than that made from dried but this is not always the case, depending on the unique properties of that specific herb. Overall, it is advised to use fresh herb material for tinctures and dried herb material for teas, infusions and decoctions as boiling water breaks down dried herb cell walls for more efficient use.

How much alcohol am I absorbing when taking a tincture and what if I am on an alcohol-free diet?

Depending on the preparation, alcohol levels might range from 25-90%. Alcohol and water are difficult to separate even if you try to evaporate the alcohol by placing in hot water. It is possible to find tinctures made with glycerin or vinegars instead of alcohol if you must, however the alcohol intake is so small in an alcohol-based tincture, it is considered to be a non-addictive amount by most physicians and practitioners.

How is a tincture administered?

The best way to administer is to place the number of drops recommended in a small amount of water or juice and drink. In acute situations, tinctures may be taken sublingually (under the tongue).

I have read about measuring "by volume" to make a tincture. What does this mean?

"By volume" refers to the balance or ratio of herb to alcohol when making a tincture. The percentage refers to the alcohol concentration in the menstruum. A simple example of this would be in a 1:5 ratio, you are using 1 part herb (gram measurement) and 5 parts alcohol (milliliter measurement).

Can I add anything to my teas to make them taste better?

Yes! You can add honey, agave nectar, a squeeze of lemon, lime or orange, broth or additional flavoring herbs like rosemary, mint or cinnamon. The protein in milk can affect the bioavailability of some herbs so milk is not highly recommended.

How safe is herbal medicine?

Herbal medicines are safe if prepared and administered properly and can have a profound effect on multiple body systems.

How effective are herbal medicines?

Efficacy is directly related to dosing and the choice of herb. Not all herbs are effective for all people. You must discover those that work with your unique body and your unique needs.

How is herbal medicine different from pharmaceutical medicine?

Many pharmaceuticals are based on a specific compound which often originates from a herb. For example, white willow bark is the herb used as the basis for the common aspirin and digitalis derived from foxglove is used for cardiac conditions. It is then chemically (scientifically) enhanced and/or altered.

Pharmaceuticals are usually targeted at one specific health issue but impact multiple body systems which is often why there are a multitude of side effects. Herbal medicines contain a multitude of medicinal components which can affect multiple pathways in the body. No herbal medicine is directed at one particular illness or issue. For example, there is no herb that is strictly used to treat sore throat or eczema. Herbs impact the full body, not just one issue or symptom. Herbal medicines do not have extensive side effects like pharmaceuticals.

Should I be afraid to take a herbal medicine as there is so much conflicting information out there, particularly on the internet?

We are living in an age of "overload" and there is so much information freely available without regulation that it's hard to know what is authentic. Be bold and try a variety of formulations to discover which herbs become allies to you in the treatment of your own unique body. As there are few side effects if any, there is little need for fear of experimenting with herbal medicines for your own needs. I recommend that when first diving into the world of herbal medicines to try simple formulations using one herb at a time. This allows you to discover which herbs work best for you. When using compounds (more than one herb in a formulation), it is hard to know which herb may be working for you and which may not.

Can I replace my pharmaceutical prescriptions with herbal medicines?

Abruptly discontinuing your current prescription medications in exchange for herbal remedies can be dangerous. If you are considering doing so, please consult a naturopathic doctor or your prescribing physician before making any changes. Reducing pharmaceuticals in favor of herbal medicines is a process and while this may be highly possible, your health and safety is most important.

What is a Clinical Herbalist?

A Clinical Herbalist requires no license, degree or certification to practice. There is no regulating body for this "career" choice or for who can practice using this title. While there are many educational workshops, programs and the like available to gain formal knowledge about herbs and the use of them, these can range from an hour to more than a year of study. Seek out a practitioner with extensive knowledge and experience with the medicinal potential of botanicals, human physiology and pathophysiology in order to provide you with a holistic and custom recommendation for your unique body and symptoms.

What is a Naturopathic Doctor?

A Naturopathic Doctor is licensed and sometimes serves under specific regulations. Often they have completed a 4-year naturopathic medical program with clinical training and have passed board exams. Herbal remedies are one of their tools in supporting a patient's health. The main things that set them apart from a Clinical Herbalist may be the depth of study (but not always) and that herbal medicine is only a part of their patient care plan.

Who uses herbal medicines?

About 4 billion people across the world use herbal medicines, according to the WHO (World Health Organization). Herbs have been used for medicinal purposes by all cultures throughout history and are used extensively in primary health care, more so in countries other than America. In America, more and more people are turning to herbal remedies as knowledge and understanding of them becomes more widely available.

What are Chinese herbal medicines?

Chinese medicines use herbs that thrive in that region of the world and often are combined with other treatments, such as acupuncture. Their history of usage goes back thousands of years with minimal side effects. Chinese herbs are often combined to form a complex formula to address a presenting health problem as well as secondary issues that may accompany it.

Can there be interactions between pharmaceuticals and herbal medicines?

Yes. It is very important to understand drug interactions with herbs as well as foods. They can often negatively interact with one another. Taking herbs and drugs at least 2 hours apart usually eliminates the cause of interaction but this is not guaranteed and therefore, you should seek the advice of your practitioner or prescribing physician.

Is there potential of overdose from taking too much of a herbal medicine?

It is recommended to only use the suggested dosage of any herbal medicine. It is rare to overdose from a herb but some have toxicity levels when taken in high doses. You must use caution as you would using any remedy or any substance in or on your unique body. It is advised to keep all herbal remedies out of the reach of children.

How many times per day should I take a herbal tincture preparation?

Average recommendation for dosage is 2-3 times per day and is sufficient even for most chronic conditions. However in some acute conditions, 4-5 times per day might be recommended though regular or extended use in high dosage amounts is usually not advised. Seek the advice of an expert before dosing adults or children.

What are the different types of herbal preparations and how do I make them?

You can make many herbal preparations in your own kitchen! They range from tinctures, teas and infusions, decoctions, oils, vinegars, salves, lotions, compresses, liniments and more.

What is the best alcohol to use as a menstruum in making a tincture?

The best alcohol to use when preparing tinctures is 80% (proof) or more, often in the form of vodka or grain alcohol. Never use any alcohol not meant for consumption like rubbing (isopropyl) alcohol. Tinctures must contain at least 25% alcohol for the purpose of preservation. General rule of thumb is: 50-60% alcohol for leafy herbs, 70-90% for fresh herbs and 80-90% for resins.

www.ingramcontent.com/pod-product-compliance
Lightning Source LLC
Chambersburg PA
CBHW071350080526
44587CB00017B/3036